ph

5.1.07

SOCIAL WORK: THE SOCIAL ORGANISATION OF AN INVISIBLE TRADE

Social Work: The Social Organisation of an Invisible Trade

Second Edition

ANDREW PITHOUSE
School of Social and Administrative Studies
University of Wales
College of Cardiff

Ashgate

Aldershot • Brookfield USA • Singapore • Sydney

Published by
Ashgate Publishing Ltd
Gower House
Croft Road
Aldershot
Hants GU11 3HR
England

Ashgate Publishing Company
Old Post Road
Brookfield
Vermont 05036
USA

British Library Cataloguing in Publication Data
Pithouse, Andrew, 1946-
    Social work : the social organisation of an invisible
    trade. - (Cardiff papers in qualitative research)
    1. Social service
    I. Title
    361.3

Library of Congress Catalog Card Number: 98-71959

ISBN 1 84014 367 3

Printed and bound by Athenaeum Press, Ltd.,
Gateshead, Tyne & Wear.

Contents

1   Preface to the second edition and an introduction
    to the study   1

2   The area office: boundaries and identities in an
    occupational world   13

3   Making social work visible: official indices and
    false trails   37

4   Issues of visibility and colleague relationships   66

5   Supervisory relations and the discreet art of
    assessment   95

6   The client: common sense theory and everyday
    practice   125

7   Telling the case: social work made visible   156

    End note: looking to the future   179

Methodological appendix   184

Bibliography   190

1 Preface to the second edition and an introduction to the study

There are a number of reasons why I thought it useful to develop a second edition of this monograph. First, the original book in 1987 contained a much reduced version of my Ph.D. The thesis examined the ways in which two teams of child care social workers in a social services department area office made their unobserved practices with children and families a visible and meaningful event to other members of the office setting. I have not sought to expand this edition with more material from the thesis. Instead, I have added some contrastive data from interviews undertaken with child care practitioners working in the very same organisational setting in late 1997, some ten years after the book was first published. Secondly, the subject matter of the text still remains relatively undeveloped in social work research. The locations, activities, relationships and meanings which constitute everyday work are not abundantly documented in welfare literature, in this regard the book may still offer itself as a useful source of ideas and concepts. Thirdly, while there has been little published in the vein of *Invisible Trade* since its first appearance (albeit there is much on ethnographic approaches to occupational settings in the Ashgate published Cardiff Papers in Qualitative Research) it is my view that much of the original text finds some resonance in the way work is conducted today and it will be seen that this is also the view of workers and managers who have contributed to this second edition.

There have of course been far reaching changes to the organisational and occupational structures of social work in the decade since the first edition. Not surprisingly then, any interest in the 'everyday world' of practice may well have been overshadowed in recent years by a more compelling and spirited debate about the very purpose and practice of social work, particularly around issues such as citizenship, profession and the political economy of welfare. Such debates continue but it is hoped that some space may be found to hear the voice of workers and managers who, as this

1

edition will illustrate, offer some important insights into what it is like to do social work in the late 1990s. For such reasons as these I hope it might not be unreasonable, nor seen as wholly self indulgent, to bring out a new edition in order to display some of the context and colour of a much neglected occupational world to a new and wider readership.

In reproducing this book I have not tried to 'write another book' whereby the original material is subjected to some fresh treatment at the hands of current theory and research. That would be absurd. The epistemological and ideological difficulties of reassembling the past in some 'ethnographic present' are well attested to (Fabian 1983; Atkinson 1996). This is not to suggest that the original work has somehow become 'sacred' or 'out of time', as if it were some anthropological construct with its subjects mythologised in quaint ritual and routine. Nor is my account of social work in the 1980s wholly out of step with contemporary practice. There is much in the book about the way work is socially organised and made visible that retains relevance for practice in the late 1990s. But the new edition will also illustrate that there are dramatic departures from what was observed in the 1980s. As we shall see, these stem from a child centred approach in a late 1990s occupational environment where paradox, unpredictability and blame appear far more pronounced than ever witnessed before.

It seemed to me that while a second edition might still be of use because of the relatively limited number of texts on this subject matter, it was more likely to enjoy a broader appeal and justification if it contained some reference to the contemporary world of work. Therefore, I approached managers and workers who operated from the same town and from the same organisational setting in which the original research took place, in order to enlist their help in this book. None of the staff who participated in the earlier research were still employed in the setting. Over the intervening years all had moved on to other jobs, or had retired. Only two remained in the organisation and they had been promoted to management positions in other parts of the social services department. In the first edition, the focus was upon all those engaged in field social work within an area office setting; this involved some fourteen qualified workers, two team leaders and an area office manager. In this edition, some ten years later, we add the views of some twenty five qualified and unqualified workers, two team managers and one senior manager who work in the same setting.

My aim was not to undertake a programme of comparative research via the same methods and theory, rather, and more simply, I wished to revitalise the text with the observations and insights of a later generation of child care practitioners. It would have proved impossible for reasons already mentioned to somehow write a new book upon the old one. But I could enliven the first edition by getting social workers and managers to read it, comment upon what they read and then contrast the world of their predecessors with their own everyday practice. Chapters were given to different groups and individuals who were asked to follow a brief checklist of suggestions on how they might examine and annotate the text in respect of the familiar and unfamiliar. Their comments were then gathered and later explored through individual interviews, except for one small group interview which arose through the preference of those particular respondents. Over thirty hours of audio taped interviews plus some brief observation and a small amount of secondary data now supply the additional material for this new edition. I have not attempted to situate the comments of these staff within some formal discourse; apart from background detail and some necessary interlocution their words stand alone in order to maximise contrast and immediacy.

Thus, we now have a text in which there is an addendum to each of the original chapters (apart from this one) containing the views of local authority social workers and their managers who provide child and family services in the late 1990s. What follows therefore is a snapshot of two generations of staff operating in the same setting and engaged with statutory child care practice informed by the (then) law and policy in England and Wales. The book intends to throw some light on what might be seen as enduring features of social organisation and it will refer to new aspects of practice which in some ways have profoundly influenced the way work is understood and carried out. If the book succeeds in displaying important continuities and contrasts it will be because of the openness, co-operation and support of staff who in the 1980s and 1990s were willing to share their experience and knowledge of what it is like to do social work and what it is like to be a social worker. This second edition is dedicated to them and to the children and families with whom they work. We now join the original text at the point where it first introduced the research setting and the methodological background to the study.

Making social work visible: an introduction to the topic

....and about five years ago I was approached by our area officer and the director to take round a journalist from the local paper for three days, showing her what it's like on the job - you know - 'a day in the life of a social worker' (laughs). Well I really planned a day that would really show her a few things! I visited loads of people, everything happened - crises, upsets, we got it all! On the move all day, in the car and out again. Then we finally got back to the office and I sat down to write it all up! She was exhausted (laughs), physically exhausted, she'd been in with me to see the clients - they were informed beforehand - and when she saw me starting to write up at half past six well that was enough! She said 'do you mind if I go now?' (laughs). So I made sure she got an idea of what it could be like but it was really not a typical day, but a day you could get now and again. Then she had to realise that all that day had to be followed through on write-ups and phone calls, you know? Oh, and the article was terrible! (laughs). What I wanted to show her was how we make decisions, how we can be faced with really difficult decisions and be so hardworked that we sometimes can't think straight. But what we got was dreadful! It was 'what a wonderful person' I was, and, 'how poor and inadequate' the clients were. It was really embarrassing. We should have had more control over it all and said 'look you can't publish that'. But, well anyway it was bad (laughs). There I was trying to show the problems and the pressures and she just got the other bit - the good social worker - you know? That's OK but I was trying to get over what the job's about and it didn't come across....

The above verbatim extract from a taped interview with a social worker conducted in the course of research for my PhD thesis aptly introduces the topic of this book. That is, an investigation of the occupational experience of doing social work and the way this is made a shared and meaningful activity for social workers in a local authority social services department. Describing these activities, as the above extract reveals, is problematic for the social worker concerned and the journalist as well. The worker understandably attempts to display the demanding and stressful nature of the occupational task. In doing so she provides a stage-managed and somewhat fictional display of everyday work. Consequently both the worker and the journalist fall into the trap of grasping work outside the usual ways that social workers in that department perceive and express their occupational experience.

As demonstrated in later chapters, social work is an inherently 'invisible' trade that cannot be 'seen' without engaging in the workers' own routines for understanding their complex occupational terrain. Social work is invisible in three particular ways. First, social workers who visit people in the privacy of their own homes or see them in the office usually do so free from observation and interference by their colleagues, who likewise pursue a similar form of intervention. Secondly, social work is invisible to the extent that the outcomes of intervention are uncertain and ambiguous; a point that will be elaborated later. Thirdly, social work is invisible in so far as practitioners do not typically retrieve and analyse the occupational processes that surround their endeavours. Like most of us they rely upon rarely stated motives and taken for granted assumptions in order to accomplish day to day routines. Thus it is no surprise that an observer, such as the journalist above, cannot 'see' what the worker wishes to be 'seen'. For only those who are accustomed to the occupational experience can appreciate what it means to do social work.

Social workers would surely forgive their colleague in the introductory extract for presenting perhaps an overly dramatic picture of the job. They too would agree that it is profoundly difficult to explain what work is really like. While habitués of the job might well recognise the issues raised in the above extract, it is likely also that the sociological reader will already have some idea of the methodological premises at work in this study and these will soon be specified. The approach here will avoid the contrived version of work presented to the above journalist and instead look to the lively and practical world of work that can only be seen by an observer who is immersed in a social work setting. For, as will be argued, it is in the organisational setting that sense is made of practice; it is here that work is 'seen' and understood. This will now be presented through a sociology that seeks to discover and analyse the social workers' typical ways for demonstrating they are engaged in appropriate practice.

The very term 'social work' remains elusive and there are no final definitions. Thus it is not the intention here to add to the many attempts within (and without) the occupation to legislate a fresh abstraction to 'fit' the uncompromisingly varied activities subsumed beneath this label. Instead a specific seam of social work will be considered, that is, the practice of child care social workers employed in a local authority social services department. The workers in question operate from an area office situated several miles from the department's main office. Like other workers in local authority departments in England and Wales, they are charged and empowered by statutory obligations in respect of child and family legislation. They also have powers to provide, at the department's discretion, various additional services for children and families.

These powers and services will be discussed in due course. However, it is essential to note at the outset that despite this shared legislative background there is variation in size, organisation and philosophy of social services departments. This makes generalisation about social work a complex and expensive venture beyond the ambitions of this study. Social services departments do not provide some standardised or divisible product. For example, they do not deliver uniform, universal or easily specifiable entitlements as with other statutory providers such as education, housing, or social security. Nevertheless, social services departments do share broadly similar organisational features such as a division of labour through case-based routines, written documentation of intervention, practitioners grouped in teams and varying degrees of service specialisation according to setting, methods, consumer category or problem.

Notwithstanding the variation to be found among social services departments, actual social work practice is frequently typified by the unobserved and uncertain nature of doing the job itself. It will be argued in later chapters that the inherent problems of visibility and uncertainty that permeate practice are resolved in the organisational setting, particularly through the social workers' individualistic and particularistic orientations towards colleagues and consumers. It will be demonstrated that social work is indelibly about particular people and problems. It is about specific identities and relationships wrought within the daily work locale. While this work locale is unique to the social workers in question it is similar to other occupational settings by dint of comparable processes that socially organise a daily world of work. To emphasise this there will be reference to literature on welfare and related occupations supporting the observations drawn in subsequent chapters.

To repeat, the subject here is the social organisation of unobserved and uncertain work. Consequently, this study focuses upon the way social work practitioners make their unseen endeavours with consumers visible to significant others in the organisation and thereby seen as satisfactory or otherwise. The form of this study will now be outlined further in respect of the research perspective employed and the sequence of topics investigated.

Research perspective

This book is based on twelve months observation of child care social workers in a social services department area office and concentrates specifically on the everyday relationships within this organisational segment. The research material was gathered by using the research method of participant observation and by conducting individual taped interviews with members of the child care teams. Reference is also made to written records and other organisational documents. However, for reasons of space, it will not be possible to reproduce all the data and related theory that supports many of the conclusions submitted in this text. A more detailed account of the research design and methodological orientation is contained in the appendix.

This study draws largely on the sociological tradition of symbolic interactionism and also includes ethnomethodological perspectives in order to recreate the core symbolic elements of life in the area office. The aim is to display as fully as possible the way that the social workers themselves perceive and create their occupational arena. In this respect the study contains orthodox and original seams of enquiry. It is orthodox in the sense that the study seeks neither to defend nor injure the interests of those who gave their trust and confidence in order that the project could be realised. Consequently, what is presented here, is the way that workers themselves understand their daily work domain. Yet the study is original in the sense that a welter of previous research including both social work and sociological sources, has conspicuously sought to construct evaluative criteria in order to assess practice, rather than explore the way workers routinely examine their own endeavours. In short, the study focuses on the orderly and mundane way that social workers make sense of their daily tasks and problems.

Social work is not short of critics and supporters who assert the effects of intervention to be either beneficial or harmful to consumers - or potentially so. Yet the world of daily practice is replete with processes that cannot be deduced from the official policy formulations of the occupation nor, for that matter, from those who locate social work within a structure of class and domination. Theories of social work as a liberal bulwark of human rights or the disguised interest of class dominion, fail to capture the subtle and often contrary world of daily practice.

There will be no attempt here to situate social work within these familiar and competing themes. Instead, the complex and often contradictory practices of people doing welfare work will be shown as the outcome of an occupational arena that demands its own specific theoretical formulation. This theory and its formulation is one that builds on the everyday meanings and understandings that are created by the social work practitioners in question. These everyday meanings and understandings will be drawn out and recast to show their specificity to situations and relationships that are contingent upon a daily work setting. It is this world of daily practical work that escapes the analytic gaze of more distanced perspectives and commentators.

This study pursues a traditional sociology of the phenomenal and immediate social world. The intention here is to reveal the organisational setting and its analysis as a process of emergent and cumulative learning: it will be shown therefore the ways in which social workers learn to make sense of their surroundings and relationships. The aim throughout will be to keep faith with the meanings and intentions of the workers in question and construe these within a theoretical and ethical perspective that acknowledges the serious enterprise called 'work'. Work, as later chapters will indicate, locates people in the midst of crucial moral currents: work is a source of esteem and worth; it is inevitably a societal measure of position and identity.

It would, of course, be possible to construct a glib critique of the social work occupation and draw ironic distinctions between prescribed and actual practice. Doubtless social work practice may sometimes offend consumers and other participants or observers. Yet this demands neither exculpation nor blame but an explanation of social workers' own largely unresearched reasons that justify what they do. Social work is a serious business with serious consequences. Not enough is known about the ways that practitioners resolve the dilemmas and unpalatable issues that permeate the occupational task. Yet it is the practitioners' typically routine resolution of these difficulties that is notably absent in the occupational and social science literature that has mushroomed around the occupation.

This gap in the literature remains partly because of the practical research difficulties of creating a lengthy association with practitioners. This is essential to gain access to rarely observed processes that only accepted members of an occupational setting can share in. Yet the gap also exists because these processes (such as assessment routines, colleague relationships, consumer typifications) have not been accorded their due significance. Researchers have all too often approached welfare settings with their own assumptions. They assess practices to the extent that they meet their own methodological designs, finding relevance in departures from these, rather than viewing actual practices as authentic constructions in themselves. This study hopes to rectify this omission. An outline of the main areas of enquiry contained in later chapters will now complete this introduction.

Sequence of topics

This study addresses the way that child care workers in an area office typically accomplish their daily routines and indicate these to be in accord with shared expectations about satisfactory work. This seemingly obvious concern with the meaning of work belies the complexity of the area office setting. Subsequent chapters will reveal the uncertain and unstable nature of the occupational endeavour and reveal the way the setting is socially organised to deal with this. The unobserved nature of practice and outcome, together with the unpredictable demands made upon practitioners by consumers, has a profound effect on the way work is understood and evaluated. Nonetheless, workers skilfully restrain a potentially chaotic occupational environment and display with considerable ease their satisfactory practice.

The social organisation of the setting is accomplished through the social workers' ability to deploy crucial assumptions that manage their turbulent work world. These assumptions derive from three broad areas of occupational experience. Briefly, these are the organisation; the collegium; the consumers. Within these major groupings lie the practitioners' means of grasping and displaying satisfactory work. These elements are daily constituted not in some mechanical fashion of a patterned occupational culture or system of values, but in the context of an emergent and socially constructed daily world. Here practitioners actively negotiate, assert, or on occasion, neglect the shared occupational assumptions that derive from working with colleagues in a welfare organisation. It is this world of day to day symbolic construction that will be revealed in the following sequence of discovery.

To begin with, social work's history resonates with issues and dilemmas in relation to the impact of organisational and professional formation. These issues will be considered in later chapters specifically from an interactionist standpoint, that is, a perspective that allows human agency authentic participation in the building and mediation of social structures. It follows that both 'organisation' and 'profession' will be construed here in the context of what the practitioners themselves mean by being a 'professional' in an 'organisation'.

The analysis provides a view of child care social work as the daily practical accomplishment of skilled members. This is not to suggest that either the 'profession' or the 'organisation' occupied by workers exists simply in the way that practitioners create their day to day work relationships. Clearly, the wider determinants of local and central government policy influence the destiny of employees in welfare bureaucracies. Thus, there is no suggestion here that social workers in their everyday work create and secure the conditions of their occupational future. Rather, they routinely construct a work-world that is not wholly given or analysable within the policies and philosophies that encode modern welfare. Policies and philosophies that are intended to direct welfare practices are mediated within the work setting and often recede into the wings of an interactive arena, where members assert their own view of appropriate practice.

The practitioners inhabit a complex and segmented occupational world. As lower participants in a large organisation they do not look to other groups within or without the organisation as a source of reference or positive alignment. Instead it will be shown (chapter two) that they secure a sense of identity and validation from their immediate colleagues in the office setting.

As members of the organisation and the occupation generally, the child care workers are faced with the shared problem of making uncertain and unobserved practice a 'witnessable' and proper activity. Hence the premise that practices may be discovered in the formal organisational criteria and indices (departmental procedures, case categories, case histories, case numbers) for processing consumers is considered. This premise is rapidly discarded as official procedures and records are discovered to be negotiated and sometimes neglected by practitioners in order to pursue their own view of appropriate work. It is shown therefore (chapter three) that the competent member of the office setting is able to manage artfully organisational rules. Indeed these dissolve into a welter of situational manoeuvres and motives that resolve the contingencies of practice. In this respect organisational procedures are the outcome of the practitioners' interpretive work and skills of negotiation. Moreover, formal procedures do not reveal the way that social workers themselves perceive and assess satisfactory practice.

The persisting theme of this study is the matter of unobserved practice and the way this is seen as appropriate or otherwise. It is discovered (chapter four) that the meaning and evaluation of work exists in the crucial realm of colleague relationships. Here, core identities and definitions about practitioners and practice are wrought that make for an orderly and predictable work world. Colleague relationships provide the template within which work is accomplished. Two processes occur that contribute to the resolution of invisibility and uncertainty. First, practitioners adopt a view of collegial competence and refrain from criticism or uninvited comment on another's practice. This reduces the possibility of competing or conflicting definitions surrounding work. Secondly, the complex and delicate task of work evaluation is left to the supervisors of the child care workers who skilfully advise, assist and sometimes intervene more directly in the way practitioners manage their work. The evaluation of unobserved practice occurs most significantly during what are known as 'supervision sessions'. Here the child care team member sits alone with the supervisor and describes her activities in relation to her cases. It is during this event that the supervisor receives a detailed account of practices and can thereby 'see' what has occurred. This display of practice through oral accounts is a simultaneous exhibition of both worker and work. It will be shown (chapter five) that a crucial way in which work is viewed as satisfactory is to 'see' the worker as the 'right' type of person for the job. This running together of doing social work and being a social worker is looked for by the team leader when she listens to and participates in accounts rendered by practitioners.

The invisibility of encounters with consumers and the outcomes of these unobserved events is rendered satisfactory or otherwise within the supervisory relationship. This relationship develops over time as social worker and supervisor increase their knowledge of the other's expectations, needs and abilities. The relationship enables both to grasp and share basic assumptions about 'good' practice. These assumptions necessarily include reference to the consumers of the service. Descriptions of consumers are an integral element of oral accounts. Such oral accounts cannot be created unless participants are aware of the typical ways of perceiving the consumers. Briefly, work cannot be made 'visible' unless rendered through shared occupational rhetoric about people, their problems and private lives.

The consumers (chapter six) are described from the viewpoint of the practitioners. In order to make sense of an often unpredictable work experience the social workers attach certain identities to those who receive the service. Social work can often be an erratic business and unanticipated demands are frequently made upon the time and skills of the workers. Furthermore, the uncertain outcomes of social work intervention can have potentially demoralising effects upon practitioners. These various hazards are described and discussed in relation to the members' usual ways of resolving occupational strains. These include shared assumptions about particular consumers and particular strategies for dealing with some of the problems they are deemed to create.

Having drawn out this work world of organisation, collegial and consumer properties there remains a final matter. This is the actual event when unobserved and uncertain practice becomes visible in oral accounts that occur during supervisory encounters. Here work is made a witnessable event and assessed as satisfactory or otherwise. These accounts are set out (chapter seven) as verbatim extracts of (taped) supervisory sessions between individual practitioners and team leaders. The accounts reveal their contextualisation in practices, relationships, identities and linguistic devices that make possible the social organisation of social work. These contextual elements will have already been the subject of previous chapters but briefly resurface in a discussion of the verbatim extracts.

Finally, it is restated that the approach adopted here is largely absent in the familiar orthodoxies that purport to support or deny the impact and legitimacy of social work. Thus, the idea that the occupation can be grasped in the purview of political economy, or in the conventional aspirations of social work's representatives, fails to recognise the issues raised here. These are the ways in which workers themselves derive their interests, motives and meanings of work from within the minutiae of daily relationships and the practical exigencies of routine work. This book attempts to shed sociological light on this neglected seam of contemporary social work.

2 The area office: boundaries and identities in an occupational world

The area office is part of a social services department that serves one of the many shire counties in England and Wales. This county contains a city, three towns and many villages and hamlets in outlying rural areas. The city and two of the towns are located on the coastline. Here, light industry and dockland provide a significant but minor source of employment. Most jobs exist in retail and service sectors in the city and coastal strip. The department's main office is located in the city and serves that population. The area office is the only detached segment of the organisation (apart from residential, day care and hospital social work staff) and serves the remainder of the county, containing a population of around one hundred thousand people. The area office is situated in a large town several miles from the department's main office in the city (this will now be referred to as the city department). The social workers in the area office serve a coastline conurbation together with rural villages and a small town several miles inland.

The social workers are organised into two child care teams and have a complement of seven practitioners in each team. Each team also has a team leader who allocates cases and supervises their practice. The two teams share an open-plan office with other workers who are grouped into two teams. One team specialises in work with people who have a mental handicap or mental illness; the other team specialises with people who have a physical handicap or who are elderly. All four teams are in close proximity and share an often noisy and busy office setting. The building also contains a floor of offices occupied by the area officer, the deputy area officer and administrative staff.

The child care workers routinely visit homes in the coastal conurbation and the inland town and villages. These localities have suffered the long-run decline of local industry (steel, coal and dockland) and endure higher levels of unemployment than the national average. Also, within these

13

localities there are higher levels of deprivation than elsewhere in the county. For example, in the areas the workers routinely visit there are less car-owners and a larger proportion of homes that have no bath or toilet facilities. There is also a higher average of elderly and elderly people living alone. Briefly, the coastal conurbation and many inland communities have in recent decades witnessed a declining economy and more recently have caught the withering blast of recession in the 1980s.

The two child care teams contain, in all, fourteen social workers, two of whom are men. All are qualified and all but three of the social workers are married. The ages of the practitioners and their length of service are typical of the occupation as a whole. For example, sixty-five per cent of fieldworkers in the profession are aged between twenty-five and forty-five years; twenty per cent are aged twenty-five to thirty years (Barclay, 1982, p.25). In the office, four of the sixteen members of both teams are in their late twenties. Two are over forty-five, the others are in the years between. In the occupation generally, seventy three per cent of fieldworkers have been in post for more than two years, forty per cent for more than five years (Barclay *op cit.*). In the child care teams most have been in their present job for more than two years, there are five 'veterans' with more than five years in post. There were three new workers recruited during the research period, one had several years experience elsewhere and the other two had recently completed training courses.

The majority of the workers in the two teams are either working mothers with grown-up families or young married women without children. They manage a busy career together with their domestic responsibilities. While there is a popular image of social workers as be-jeaned, youthful and of unkempt appearance (see Crabtree, 1981, p.9) the child care workers clearly challenge this notion. They are casually but smartly dressed and particular attention to appearance is paid when they attend court or other functions where they officially represent the office and department. Indeed, if there were a stereotype of social workers as reasonably well-heeled, energetic, middle or lower middle-class, female and conventionally dressed, then this image would more faithfully reflect the office membership.

The two child care teams hold some six hundred cases between them. A case is the basic organisational unit that is intended to document a specific service to a particular consumer. It is a written history of activities in respect of consumer and social worker and concerns matters in relation to the specialist practices of the team. Thus in the area office there are in total some one thousand five hundred active cases. Twelve per cent of these are held by the team dealing in services for people with a mental illness or handicap, forty-eight per cent of cases are managed by the team dealing

14

with elderly or physically handicapped people, and forty per cent of cases involve child and family related services. However, it is these child care workers and their cases that concern this study. That is, how do they make their unobserved visits to people in the above localities a visible and satisfactory endeavour? The following comments on occupational boundaries and identities provide an initial answer to this question and offer further clues with which to pursue this central topic.

The area office: insulation and control

The image of the social services department represented here is some distance from traditional occupational homilies upon professions as groups bounded by shared values and objectives. Instead there will be a description of an organisation that is segmented, insulated at various levels, and where control of practice is subtly contested. It will be shown that the workers in the area office draw their occupational identity and inspiration from immediate colleagues and not from the department. Nor do they look to external bodies such as professional associations or trade union representatives, except on rare occasions. This aspect of office relationships with the parent department will be discussed before proceeding to relationships with external networks and other agencies.

A great deal of social policy and occupational literature looks to the legislative, organisational and philosophical underpinnings of welfare services. This describes largely what the service is *for* rather than what it is *like*. Similarly, sociological analyses have frequently viewed practitioners as derivatives of professional and bureaucratic role formation. Their behaviour is conceived as a response to the patterned stimuli of internalised norms and organisational procedures. Social workers' orientations have been viewed as fixed and few, whereas it will be argued here that practitioners have a range of responses and manoeuvres which they actively construct. It is essential therefore to conceive of the worker as one who makes choices and creates adaptive strategies in order to accomplish work. The new recruit (like the researcher) first learns the ropes of organisational life. She or he has to acquire and deploy the shared meanings that make sense of the complex organisational terrain. In brief, the recruit is socialised into the organisational culture.

Organisational socialisation entails the cognitive mapping of a social system (Manning, 1979b). This is not simply learning about the objects in a setting such as colleagues, equipment, formal rules and so forth, it also includes learning the temporal and spatial dimensions surrounding these elements in the organisation. There is, as Van Mannen and Katz (1979)

15

observe, an invisible landscape to organisational environments. Thus, members of a setting must learn temporal aspects such as how much time to spend on certain tasks, when to approach colleagues, how long to spend on breaks and when to leave work. Similarly, organisational space concerns the way members learn where they fit or connect with other elements or colleagues in a setting. Briefly, the social workers in question, like others in a complex organisation, develop their own institutional map of perceived organisational properties. Like others in complex organisations (see Strauss *et al.,* 1964, p.354) they develop shared conceptions of organisational boundaries, internal locales and group loyalties.

The area office is a segment of the social services department. The term 'segment' is located in an interactionist perspective that emphasises conflict and competition over differing interests among professionals in organisations (see Bucher and Strauss, 1961; Bucher and Stelling, 1969; Heraud, 1971). Segment implies a notion of groups in continual and spontaneous process and actively asserting or protecting their local interests. Here elements within the organisation engage in claims for recognition and frequently negotiate the formal rules and objectives of the organisation in favour of specific groups. The following account of the area office and its relationships with the city department draws on this notion of groups involved in processes of negotiation and competition. It will be shown that members have mapped out the perceptual boundaries around their segment and continually attempt to repair these in order to fend off intrusions from the departmental hierarchy.

In the course of the research I attended monthly meetings of the entire area office establishment. These take place in the open-plan office and the area manager or his deputy usually chair the proceedings. Typically there is reference by the manager to some new administrative procedure but there are also frequent comments made on more local matters. For example, meetings often commence with news about important events in the lives of staff members present and past. This local and more 'domestic' account of 'births deaths and marriages' among the staff and those who have left but are remembered, implicitly affirms an 'office' identity. New recruits are 'officially' welcomed by the managers at these meetings. Similarly, those who may soon be leaving are gently eased towards a new shift in their personal or occupational career. Here a warm farewell and commemorative card or gift marks the event.

These routine ovations of collegial concern help stake out the boundaries of the occupational group. Such warm affect is rarely reserved for higher management. For example, at one meeting new instructions were issued in respect of especially long journeys made to visit clients (such as children placed in care outside the county). New forms now had to be completed before the visit and permission sought from management. The news, delivered by the office manager, was received with snorts of derision by the social workers who were affronted by the implication that they were not the best judge of how to plan their visits and movements. These points were expressed at the meeting and one worker loudly stated that such long-distance visits were sometimes urgent and anticipatory form-filling was not always possible:

child care worker:	These mileage forms are stupid! You don't always know when you'll visit, er you know - it could be a crisis and you have to go!
area manager:	(nods) I agree. Look, if we scrap this one (form) they'll (higher management) only invent another one. In fact they want to scrap all out-of-county visiting and have social workers in those areas doing the visiting, so we don't want to give them the opportunity of changing our ways of working.
team leader:	But visiting the client wherever they are is a principle of the way we work, why don't they (higher management) understand this?
area manager:	I appreciate your point completely. But I don't think we ought to rock the boat on this one. We'll go along with it and you tell me when you come to do a visit or if it's immediate we can work something out. I don't think we need to worry about this one....

There followed several comments pointing to a shared concern that the department were always trying to restrict the use of resources and complicate matters through administrative routines. Changes in procedure such as the one above are frequently submitted and commented on at the monthly area office meetings. This provides the participants with an opportunity to affirm their distinctive local identity through an almost ritual criticism of higher management. This is not unique to the office in question. Observation of other social work offices suggests that practitioners are interested in the organisation to the extent that it affects them negatively (Satyamurti, 1981, p.188). Also, that a veritable 'Berlin Wall' exists between managers and practitioners in some social work departments has been noted by Parsloe (1981, p.92). Similarly, workers have complained in many welfare settings about the layers of decision-making, particularly in relation to major child care problems (Barclay, 1982, p.127-8).

Yet, it is equally evident that social work organisations do not always impinge upon workers as much as their complaints would indicate. Indeed, it has been suggested that some practitioners have too much freedom and discretion (Barclay 1982, p.131). In the office setting the social workers do not complain of ponderous chains of command, indeed they attempt to keep their contacts with the department to a minimum. Among the child care workers there is an embracing perception that all administrative regulation detracts from the 'real' work of visiting consumers. There is a marked similarity between their work orientations and those of other lower participants who work in organisations that process peoples' problems. For example, Manning notes that beat policemen invoke an 'individualistic' and 'entrepreneurial' work ethic unhindered by administrative routine as the ideal activity:

> ....only the everyday activities of the constable even approach the forms and function of 'real police work'. Paper work, court appearances, administrative tasks or report writing....are considered ex post-facto glosses upon real work on the ground. (Manning, 1977, p.269).

In the area office, administrative work is perceived as an intrusion and higher management the culprits of this diversion from 'real' work. Yet throughout the research there were no administrative directives or schemes advanced that sought to control closely the daily movements and practices that the workers individually produced. Daily work is very much a matter of workers responding to demands rather than initiating services in relation to their cases. Nevertheless they visit consumers according to priorities they set themselves. They apply their own preferred modes of intervention: that is, the skills and relationships they feel most comfortable with. They ration their time and pace their energies in light of their own experience of case requirements. While they respond to the erratic demands made upon them, they do so with scant interference from supervisors, managers or team colleagues. All these points will be developed in later chapters, at this juncture it need only be said that work itself does not occur in some standardised and easily monitored sequence of time and event.

Furthermore, in the office there are no formal attempts to check or scrutinise day to day practice apart from supervision meetings with the team leader and these occur fortnightly or monthly in some instances. In general the qualified child care worker is left to get on with her cases free of any direct intrusion by her immediate colleagues and superiors. It is this basic element of day to day autonomy that workers take for granted. It is the basis upon which the job is routinely done. It is from this position they view all changes in the organisation, hence administration in any shape or form is viewed as an unwarranted distraction or managerial threat to their accustomed self-regulation.

While social workers may have little or no control over the range of practical services and resources that can be provided to consumers (residential, day care, nursery provision, finance) they nevertheless enjoy considerable self regulation of their own activities. In the office the child care workers have learned they can create, expect and enjoy a certain day to day control of their own work. Their self-directed activities become a common-sense fact of organisational life, taken for granted. In turn this becomes a tacit rarely-stated assumption and part of their cognitive map. Such a map is a way of seeing which, as Manning (1979b, p.209) suggests, 'provides the matrix for all deliberate considerations without itself being deliberately considered'. Hence, practitioner self-regulation remains largely unanalysed in the social workers' rhetoric and criticism of the organisation. Yet it is because workers enjoy substantial space to manage their own practices that administrative directions are promptly cast as intrusive and restraining. Thus, simply noting the negative commentary about the department would lead a researcher (and reader) to a skewed understanding of the occupational experience of the area office. It was possible to explore more accurately the extent of departmental restriction in the first series of taped interviews with managers and practitioners.

Maintaining boundary and distance

In the course of gathering interviews it became apparent that members of the area office held no positive attachment for the main organisation in the city. Most responses indicated the beneficial effects of their geographic and social distance from the city department. Thus, the department as a whole, cannot be described in terms of some 'professional community' (Goode, 1957) of consensual service ideals. Instead the area office represents a segment that carefully manages its local affairs in such a way as to prevent close scrutiny by the departmental hierarchy. For example, the city department depends upon reports and day to day telephone communication to monitor events in the detached area office. This gives the local management an opportunity to manage skilfully the exchange of information between themselves and the city department:

> area manager: ....yes we are some distance from the department but I enjoy it. But it's good and bad. You see we can control the information that goes to them as we represent the office. They never come here to see what we do, but on the other hand, we are removed from contact and we can't influence things so much.

While the local managers are somewhat removed from the spheres of influence in the city department they can at least 'control the information'. This ability to be the 'gatekeeper' of delicate and potentially damaging information is described below by the manager. He reveals how, in the past, he has actively sought a degree of local autonomy and protection of his staff from scrutiny by higher management:

> area manager: ....I fight tooth and nail to keep the identity of the office. I might criticise people in the office, I would never criticise them outside or allow their files (case records) to go to (higher) management without me. These privileges I've had to win. In (city department) a social worker can be sent for without their manager or team leader knowing....and he's up there with the Director explaining his actions - I won't have that and they know that. We're really a true detached office and our staff want to keep it that way.

The area office manager and deputy are keen guardians of their hard won local autonomy. In this sense the office is part of a complex organisation that contains negotiable working arrangements that have emerged from the initiatives of participants and not through formal rules or objectives. The setting in many respects reflects the views of Strauss *et al.* (1963, p.165). They observe that complex organisations obtain order through the continual

20

reconstruction of relationships stemming from processes of compromise, informal agreements and local discretion that is often hidden from higher administrators.

Interviews with the child care workers reveal similar perspectives. They too asserted the need for a well managed distance from the city department and all commented on the belief that higher management are 'out of touch', unappreciative of 'real social work' and concerned only with undue restriction of their local activities. In their view their own day to day endeavours with consumers are the authentic realm of work and not their membership of a distanced department and the completion of their administrative requirements. 'Real' work is their face to face contact with service users and the deployment of their preferred skills and methods of intervention.

Workers' accounts of managerial dereliction have been cast by some occupational observers as unconscious displacement of the inherent anxieties of the job (Parsloe, 1981, p.92) or evidence of practitioner immaturity (see Scott, 1969, pp.101-110). However, if we view organisational disaffection only as intra-personal defences or deficiencies we lose sight of more compelling arguments. These include organisations as made up of segments in competition. Thus if social work settings are frequently contested environments then we would do better to search for the cause of this in structuring properties of organisational division and differentiation and not in some collective psychological impairment among the practitioners. In the area office for example, the social workers see themselves as separate from and 'superior' to the city department, this came across in most interviews:

child care worker: ....we're very much superior. I think we all feel superior, more organised and efficient than the people at (city department). They don't seem to find any advantage in being that much closer to management. We can get on with things down here without too much trouble. It's rather nice that we're removed....

In the area office the workers see themselves as the definers of good practice and their comments about higher management are a means of asserting this shared perception of their occupational location. Gossip and criticism are a means of informal social control (Coser, 1961) and it would be possible to submit at this point many accounts by practitioners about the

21

shortcomings of higher management. However, my concern is not to document the innumerable stories offered by social workers that serve to cast them as 'heroes' and the management as 'villains'. Rather I wish to suggest that such accounts (accurate or otherwise) are not psychological defence mechanisms but more plausibly a means of asserting a right to a cherished autonomy. This autonomy is rarely specified but remains a tacit base upon which stories are formulated by members of a close colleague group. Observations of other occupations engaged in welfare (Blau and Scott, 1963, p.73) and health care (Bennis *et al.*, 1958) indicate how social workers and nurses look to their immediate colleague group as a resource for offsetting the impact of administrative intrusions. In the area office the workers look to their team colleagues as a source of reference for 'good work'. The higher management are seen as practically and morally estranged from everyday practice and hence unqualified to impose legitimate criteria for processing work.

Despite the readily available criticism of the city department as overly 'bureaucratic' it was apparent from observation and interviews that practitioners enjoy substantial self-direction over their day to day activities. Their social distance from the main department is recognised by all and carefully maintained by local management. As 'gatekeepers' the managers are keen to stress that overt and hostile criticism of the city department might invoke a more interested gaze by higher administrators towards their local activities. Thus criticism of the department would never arrive there, if at all, in its original abrasive form. The department hierarchy, like other 'high ups' receive distilled information that barely reveals the feelings or climate of opinion lower down the organisation (see Merton, 1968, p.401). Thus the local managers take practitioners' complaints and refine them into constructive suggestions; there is an adept mediation of information described as follows:

area manager: I respect and protect the staff....you see I don't stop complaints going through to (city department) as long as they're thought out - nothing hysterical. I don't allow that. Now, if management send memos that would really upset the social workers I would take it back and say is this really necessary? We try to recognise problems before they occur. I don't spend a lot of time at (city department) but I spend long enough to pick up

what's going on - you know - someone's
onto something - and I've then got our
answers ready for them when they start
asking questions! That often keeps the
pressure off social workers....

This extract again indicates the guarded and segmented character of the
area office. The careful handling of information and communication helps
create an insulated office with a colleague group who look to themselves
and not the wider department for their reference to satisfactory practice.
The child care workers have learned that it is the office and not city
department that is the source of their satisfaction. A negative view of the
hierarchy prevails and a shared emphasis upon quiet insulation and skilled
control of communication characterises their contact with the department.
Within the area office collegial solidarity and harmony typify the overt
relationships between practitioners. The implications of these consensual
forms for the way work is shared and assessed will be discussed in later
chapters. At this point it would be essential to complement the above
account of organisational separation and insulation with references to the
way practitioners see their relationships with other agencies that they
routinely contact. This will indicate that in these external relationships the
workers also engage in manoeuvres that protect their autonomy and self-
image as correct definers of practice.

Outsiders and the colleague group: strategies of control

The social worker is at the periphery of her organisation and interacts with
numerous occupational groups that make up the apparatus of state and
voluntary welfare. As Whittington (1983, p.266) notes, the worker is part of
a 'boundary spanning network'. Yet, lodged in the imagination of related
occupations (health, education, police, legal system) and the lay public is a
jumbled image of social work's purpose and practices. Furthermore, other
occupational groups have their own guarded practices and traditions which
militate against the smooth coordination of disparate welfare services (see
Dingwall and Eeklaar, 1982, p.18,22).

That there are problems of communication and coordination between
social workers and related occupations is a familiar enough theme to all
involved. Less familiar is the way in which these relationships are routinely
managed. Observations in the area office revealed that the child care
workers frequently shared stories about other agencies that would highlight
some unsatisfactory aspect of practice by these external groups. The telling

of stories is a feature of organisational life that has been noted in other occupations that deal with complex social problems and have to interact with other agencies (see Dingwall, 1977 on health visitor training). Essentially, such stories help to bolster the occupational self-image. Indeed, all occupations face the problem of making their tasks appear important to themselves and to those outside (Hughes, 1958). This telling of stories confers significance upon the teller and the listener(s) and provides both with a sense of membership and esteem.

Such stories are all the more important to groups that have to undertake unpleasant duties that threaten a sense of self worth and status. For example, Emerson and Pollner (1975) note how members of a psychiatric emergency team engaged in 'dignifying rationalisations' that helped them justify the fact that they had to incarcerate people in institutions that were not exactly harbours of care and therapy. Likewise, in the area office it was possible to note frequent stories of 'incompetent' hospital consultants, 'indifferent' GP's and 'unhelpful' policemen who had no idea of the distressful decisions and unenviable tasks that the social workers had to manage - such as taking a child into care or handling an urgent hospital admission.

Yet interview data revealed that the child care practitioners have no distinctly shared orientation to other agencies. Some workers were, by their own admission, better than others at winning support and approval from related occupations. This has much to do with the entrepreneurial and individualistic nature of case-based social work whereby workers routinely created specific relationships with other agencies and individuals:

child care worker:	....let me give you an example. When we go to court I don't think we're held in high esteem *but* (her emphasis) personality and status come into it....If they know who you are and connected with, it comes through. For example, I was given £25 by the Rotary Club because the secretary's wife is on the bench of the (local) juvenile court and knows me and thinks I'm a reasonable person. So I get £25 (for a client)....you see you have to prove yourself to them....

Quite who 'them' are depends very much on the worker in question. Interviews indicated very different perceptions of the same occupation held by members of the same team. For example, a majority of one team thought they had generally poor relations with the police:

> ....the police see us as softies and er with all due respect to the police I would tell them as much as I think safe. My feeling is the police always want to get their man, that's their role....

Yet three members of the same team offered different responses, as one said:

> Er, I think the police appreciate us more than others do. I get on with them and I think they see us doing the same thing as them - we help keep the community stable....

In brief, most child care workers cited particular agencies they had problems with and here the courts and police were frequently mentioned. This may not be surprising given the occupational experience of a 'law and order' backlash directed at social workers (Pearson, 1978) and criticism by police and courts of social workers as ineffective, inexperienced and sometimes subversive (see Punch, 1979, p.109; Johnson, 1980; Smith, 1979). The child care workers also have reservations about health service staff. While several spoke of good relationships with health visitors and GP's, they seemed to share the view held by other workers that doctors view social workers as subordinates who will deliver a service on demand (Stevenson and Parsloe, 1978, p.265; Mattinson and Sinclair, 1980, p.282; Satyamurti, 1981, p.104).

child care worker: GPs expect us to act at their beck and call, like the health visitors do. But I resist this. They make it clear what they think of us - not very much - but their referrals often don't have very much to do with the service. They get on their high horse but we're firm with them....

It is not the intention to document here the many and varied stories about the shortcomings of related occupations. What can be detected from observation and interview is the feeling that the workers see themselves used as a 'dustbin' for other agencies' problems. Furthermore, these agencies sometimes expect their demands to be met immediately and also attempt to specify the type of service required. The workers resolve this demeaning experience in two ways. First, workers attempt to maintain control over their relationships with these agencies by building rapport and co-operation with specific individuals. This entrepreneurial activity of getting the best out of other related occupations through personal contacts is recognised by all workers and they all speak of the need for skills of persuasion and communication.

Secondly, no single worker is satisfied with *all* the agencies she deals with. Consequently every worker can share to some extent in the daily experience of social work as misunderstood or under suspicion. Hence collective strategies of denying the validity of other agencies can be discerned in shared stories of occupational irregularities by outside groups. This practitioner labelling of people in other related agencies as 'heroes, villains or fools' represents a feature of social control in most group interaction (see Klapp, 1954). It is a means of maintaining crucial sentiments about self and group identity. However, these ascriptions are not fixed and people may move from 'fool' to 'hero'. Thus, while specific occupations are looked upon with distaste, it is the case that specific members of them may become 'heroes' and enjoy the confidence extended to team colleagues.

Like other social workers (Dunham, 1980; Currie, 1982) the child care workers are well aware of the discrediting attacks upon their occupation by other occupations and the 'unduly vindictive and sensational' attention of the media (Barclay, 1982, p.166). In the face of this they experience a threatened identity and a sense of occupational stigma. Stigma, as a concept of spoiled identity, has been more commonly employed in reference to the consumers of welfare (Pinker, 1971). However, it clearly has relevance for social work practitioners in terms of occupational prestige and acclaim.

It should be remembered that notions of occupational competence and status are not fixed but are continually fought for and claimed in processes of competition and conflict (see Bucher and Stelling, 1977, p.123). Social work is no different. Social workers have been attacked by some educationalists for providing an ineffective service (Brewer and Lait, 1980) and in respect of child abuse there is public scepticism about their ability to protect adequately children at risk. Whatever the merit of these criticisms there is presently a climate in which 'bashing social workers is an acceptable political game' (Shearer, 1980, p.16). Given these widespread assumptions together with an audience of related occupations perceived as unsympathetic, it is understandable if child care workers experience a sense of stigma.

The workers in the area office do perceive threats to their occupational identity and they offset these by techniques of neutralisation (Matza and

Sykes, 1957). That is, they deny their critics any competence to judge their activities. Only those who really 'know' what day to day work is all about can understand or comment on the occupational task. The practitioners deal with a stigmatising environment by drawing their occupational boundaries tightly around the area office and the immediate team. An esprit de corps of embattled welfare veterans is created as a bulwark against outside groups who must be suffered, manipulated, ignored or subtly educated in the ways of social work.

The workers believe that their endeavours do not fall neatly into simple categories of success. Their interventions in the lives of children and families resist easy assessment and the risk of failure is always expected in dealing with child care problems. Consequently the workers look inwards to those who intimately share in this specific occupational experience. Hence, they draw their organisational perimeters to include those close colleagues in the team and office in order to resist the intrusions of the city department and other agencies. The area office and the team become a laager for a beleaguered membership. It is here in the office setting that the workers seek a sense of occupational worth and validation of their social work practice.

Summary: the office as a social world

The colleague group of child care team mates and other office members acts as a reference group, not simply by dint of physical location, but, as Shibutani (1955, p.567) states, as a locus of 'effective communication'. Shibutani's use of reference group describes a communication system which has developed a special world-view that accentuates the difference between those in and out of the collectivity. This aptly applies to the area office whereby those 'outside' (city department, other agencies) are viewed as ineligible to assess the service or the worthy efforts of the membership. The workers are 'locals' (Gouldner, 1957) in the sense that they look to the office for a sense of purpose and esteem. They transform the office into a 'social world': that is, a structure of meanings and relationships that provide secure boundaries and a creditable identity.

The area office is a social world that provides both spatial and perceptual reference for the meaning of work. This concept of 'world' is one that offers a view of creative members who are not over-constrained by the limits of their organisational setting (see Strauss, 1978, p.120). Thus, so far the members of the office have been introduced in the context of world-building and purposive practitioners. The notion of 'world' emphasises aspects of negotiation, process, identity and communication and these aptly reflect some of the themes discussed so far. For example, the office membership carefully negotiates its relations with the parent department. Their negative but careful orientation towards the city department, rather than depicting strict regulation of practice and procedures, stands as implicit praise of local arrangements. The entrepreneurial, case-based activity of self-directing workers is the largely realised and defended practice of the office.

The temporal and experiential process of working in the office socialises the workers into a close-knit collegial group. The socially competent member of this setting learns that she looks to her office and team companions for support and definition of appropriate practice. Alternative attempts from external agencies to shape the service are resisted. Aware of their poor image in the eyes of related occupations the members defend themselves against a bruised and stigmatised identity. The sharing of stories, accounts and tales of deficiency in would-be critics helps repair a collective notion of competent practitioners. Through these group processes a social world is constructed to provide reference for the meaning of practice and a convivial setting for a sometimes embattled work force. Apart from these shared strategies, individual workers employ their own talents to persuade significant others in the city department and related agencies to support their viewpoint over the way practice should be accomplished.

So far the social world of day to day work has been mapped through the child care workers' routine perceptions of boundaries and identities. This has introduced the practitioners in terms of who they are and where they 'live' occupationally. The next step is to examine how they accomplish daily work. We now embark on an exploration of the office itself and it will be shown that the themes of negotiation, identity, conflict and communication, introduced above, play a profound part in the meaning of work. It is here in the office setting, among close colleagues, that sense is made of their uncertain and contested endeavours.

Ten years later

On returning to the research setting a decade later there were many new features in service structure and culture to contemplate - yet at the same time it was evident that the day to day world of practice held some familiar landmarks despite the many changes in the 1990s that have transformed UK social welfare. First impressions revealed an open plan office (like before) with clusters of desks, some with computers holding client records (unlike before), an erratic flow of workers entering and leaving the office throughout the day sharing easy banter while selecting some particular confidant for a discreet exchange, or joining with some small knot of colleagues that would form and dissolve quickly once the business at hand had been shared (like before). These brief encounters between members of the setting were the backdrop to the main activity of desk-bound paperwork and phone calls that seemed so reminiscent of the office observed in the 1980s. Then as now, workers seemed to be best characterised as solo practitioners, getting on with their own cases while enjoying the 'groupness' of the setting - almost required by the nature of the task to be 'gregarious loners', eager to engage with others but ultimately isolated by their own caseload and the singular duties this called forth. This surface view of work was quickly recognised by the workers who read this chapter and who saw much similarity between the two periods:

> ....yes, the chapter sits very well indeed today - we are in our own social world here - there is a sense of 'us' - I can see a lot from then to now....but there's been a lot of change as well....

The most obvious departure lay in the structure of the teams themselves. While covering the same geographical boundary as before they had been realigned from two teams visiting different patches but dealing with similar sorts of cases, to a short term team and a long term team serving the overall population. As before, the bulk of the clientele lived in the main town. The two team leaders and fourteen or so practitioners of ten years ago had been replaced by two team managers (note, 'manager' not leader). The short term team manager supervised seven full time qualified workers, two social work assistants and three family carers. Attached to this team were three staff who acted as permanent duty workers located in the reception area which was also home to administrative staff. These duty staff were gatekeepers to the office dealing with a variety of callers and problems which came directly to the door as well as by phone and fax machine. In accepting a referral they would be aware of department criteria over priorities, notably, those issues where harm or risk of harm existed for a child which warranted a full and immediate investigation, or, where there was concern over a child's welfare that was not urgent but required further enquiry as soon as possible. Should the referrals become active cases these would be held by the short term team for a maximum of six months and thereafter handed on to the long term team.

The long term team manager supervised seven full time qualified social workers and four unqualified social work assistants and one family carer.

There were five additional family carers who were part-time and paid on a sessional basis. Ten years ago there were very few unqualified social work assistants and there were no staff described as family carers. Other than this, there were the same number of qualified practitioners in both teams as before. Similarly, the majority of staff were women. And exactly as before, there were only two male staff, both qualified social workers. A major difference as we shall see in later chapters is that the unqualified staff do the direct 'care' work with families while the qualified workers are more engaged in investigative work followed up by what many described as a case management approach.

While none of the workers in the setting had participated in the original study many had been in practice since the late 1980s and most had joined the department in the early to mid 1990s. They were aware of working in a fast changing environment that had given rise to far more discomfort if not uncertainty than that experienced by their forbears over the impact and purpose of child care practice. The story is familiar to a readership aware of the seismic upheavals in social work that have challenged the optimistic promise of a more communitarian form of child and family welfare envisioned in the modernising reforms of welfare in the 1970s. Like other workers, this generation had experienced decentralisation, de-layering of management, the all consuming focus over child safety and risks therein, the shift to greater openness and accountability over user involvement and the gradual if inevitable adoption of case management as the core mode of intervention. Such events, identified by most respondents, had exercised a dramatic influence on practice which in turn placed increasing expectations upon the setting and membership as the source of support and daily satisfactions.

In brief, their occupational world compared with that of ten years ago had become more tightly bounded by four particular events: specialisation, decentralisation, the pressing demands of child protection practice and local government reorganisation. In combination, these produced a setting less permeable and negotiable than before, making the world of daily social work more stressed and internal than could ever have been anticipated a decade ago. An outline of key changes in demographic and organisational characteristics will now provide some essential context. First demographic events. In 1997 the two teams served a population of around 120,000 people, an increase of about 5 per cent from a decade before. Over this period the age structure of 0-4 year olds in the area remained virtually constant while there had been a three percent decrease in children aged 5-15 years. The percentage of those unemployed had fallen by 1.2 per cent over the decade whereas the proportion of the population economically active had risen by 3 per cent; behind this figure lay a marked decrease in men working and far more women employed in the low paid service sector. During this period the number of one and two person households had increased and those households containing three to five persons had dropped from fifty to forty per cent. At the same time, lone parent households had shown a marked rise. Such population and household characteristics are not inconsistent with UK trends. The two child care teams of the late 1990s were dealing with broadly the same size of population but with fewer families with two plus children, more lone parent households, more women in work, and more men unemployed than a decade before.

Key organisational changes comprise the following. Ten years ago there was an area office containing two child care teams and two generic adult teams covering a small town and a large rural area. There was an area officer and a deputy. Decentralisation led to the area office being closed in the late 1980s and staff were separated geographically into more specialised team-based settings covering mental health, older people and physical disability, learning disability, child care. Teams were located in different parts of the town and outlying rural area. The two child care teams were rehoused in smaller offices in the same location and continued to serve the same patch.

The loss of the area office and its larger membership of practitioners meant that the child care workers were now part of a much smaller group and one which still felt no great sense of attachment to the city department several miles away. This diaspora of teams and resources dotted around the county were each managed by a principal officer who linked up, by specialism, with a small cadre of senior management at city department. Thus from a large central department with one area office there became a system of satellite offices populated with small groups of specialist staff with devolved control of most day care and residential resources in their immediate area. Middle and upper management in their various functional strata were de-layered via early retirement or through relocation to the many specialist patch based teams, taking responsibility for all provision within that locality. Management, as the essential ingredient in any 'them and us' attitude held by practitioners was simply no longer concentrated as before. There was now only a lean directorate of half a dozen senior officers in the city department. In short there were precious few of 'them' upon which to heap reproach for the state of things and hence a lot more focus on 'us' as the source of most solutions and, as we shall see later, some discontent.

Within the city department, specialisation, decentralisation, devolution of resources were, as elsewhere, cast as wholly good and progressive, leading, it was assumed, to more effective practice and closer relations with users. This was the rationale and it undoubtedly achieved much in the view of most respondents. Yet, it inevitably increased a sense of vulnerability by placing staff in settings that were sometimes experienced as small, dispersed, insulated and hard pressed places of work with little sense of critical mass as an organisation and the sense of security that this can engender. Thus while the city department was viewed a decade ago by the two teams as distanced yet potentially intrusive it was nonetheless there as an entity to be negotiated, exploited or avoided. Now there was no 'centre' to speak of, instead there was a small directorate which saw its purpose as policy development and strategic planning rather than operational decision making. The stripping out of management and the devolution of resources and decision making to local teams while 'empowering' to some extent for staff and users, nonetheless created a feeling of isolation for many.

To repeat, for many workers, 'going local' in specialist teams was often perceived as going small and vulnerable. This was compounded by the impact of two major external events. The first of these, and perhaps the most compelling influence upon practice and occupational culture, has been the ascendancy in the UK of child protection as a more investigative and policing function which, according to many critics, has supplanted a more supportive family focused practice. This familiar debate needs no elaboration here, however, what will be seen in later chapters is the way in which the careful management of risk in relation to children's safety and parental misconduct, as well as worker and agency protection from blame, has brought significant change to supervisory roles, collegial relations and office culture.

The second major event, local government re-organisation in England and Wales, also made a dramatic impact on the setting. In 1996, the county split into two new unitary authorities. The child care workers now found themselves still decentralised and specialist but in a very much smaller authority and social services department. Before, they were in a large organisation and were one of several child care teams. Now, they were *the* major child care provider in a much shrunk department. Some instability around management had also arisen in the months before and during the break up of the county when the team had seen the arrival and departure of three principal officers. After re-organisation they enjoyed the more permanent appointment of a manager whose remit covered all child care social work operations in the new small authority. This officer together with three others (responsible for residential care, fostering, child protection administration) comprised the entire middle management accountable to an assistant director and director of social services. However, eighteen months after reorganisation the workers found themselves without an assistant director (made redundant and post deleted) and a director who had decided to take early retirement. These events led the practitioners to assume that there was little purpose in looking anywhere but to themselves for guidance and leadership. As one worker said:

> ....It feels like that line in an old song - 'there's no one here but us chickens'...and we're such a small authority now, there's no management to speak of, they're (the new smaller directorate) er...well what is their relevance for us? You see we were the backwater of a bigger authority before, now we're nearer the centre and a major part of the new department - but the carping still goes in the same direction (directorate) although there's hardly anyone there!

In this context the office became an even more intense social world, one where hierarchy in the form of the two team managers and the externally based but frequently visiting middle manager were largely 'it' as one of them said. In such a compressed structure and one where child protection remained an ever present source of anxiety, the role of managers became even more critical and subject to the sometimes ambivalent gaze of staff:

> Because there's so few in management here they are inevitably more powerful and because of the way we work here on child protection stuff they are forever involved in your cases. But at the same time they are so busy that it's hard to get a few minutes of their time. It's funny but what we need is more management, more effective management that can handle the uncertainties and place more trust in us....

For this respondent there was, as for many in the office, a concern that the spectre of child abuse involved not only assessing risk to a child's safety but also the risk arising from practising in a wider 'blame culture' in which both worker and agency might find themselves the subject of serious criticism from without, deserved or otherwise. Hence, the frequent interest of team managers in case decisions and related progress. While some found this unwelcome other respondents found it a useful and acceptable process of scrutiny in which they could share accountability rather than control of decisions. This point was thoughtfully put by one recently qualified worker with two years experience:

> In a sense we are all managers now, we're all in a line of resource management and I'm really a case manager, I make decisions and I make sure I check with (team manager) because I don't want to leave something out and then it lands on me! It's about task oriented child safety, that's what we do. The concept of care has gone. Others do that. I manage resources, and I need support from my manager, guidance, not control - it's all management what we do and I'm the middle person....

This much changed world of worker supervision will occupy later chapters, at this point it can be noted that one fixed landmark remained the office as a locus of support and security much as before, perhaps more so in a volatile and shrinking organisational world. Now, the only management to whom some ritual abuse could be exported were no longer safely outside but inside the office for the most part. The source of administrative control, made even more intense in recent years because of the shift of practice towards child protection, meant that monitoring, decision making and other aspects of worker regulation no longer emanated from 'out there' in the upper reaches of a department but were now much more driven from within the office and by staff themselves as much as from management:

> We've got quite strong self regulation as a group - it values itself - but affection disappears as it goes up, apart from the assistant director who has disappeared! (made redundant)....And we're not a homogeneous group here (office setting), there are conflicting dynamics - we're more warm within small groups and networks rather than simply because someone's your team mate....

A strong sense of boundary around the office and selected colleagues still seemed to obtain, perhaps more heightened than before because of the nature of child protection work. Such work involves more than ever before collaboration with other agencies. The question now arises as to how closely the office boundary is reinforced or made permeable by its encounters with other professionals, notably health visitors, nurseries, schools, and the police. Ten years before, other agencies were treated with some suspicion because they were considered unsympathetic, ignorant or disruptive of child care practice. A decade later the situation had altered markedly. The coming of multi-agency practice and planning in child protection had made significant inroads into the old assumption that somehow child care workers are alone and unloved. For example, the police, seen by the child care workers of the 1980s as the unlikeliest of partners in welfare, were now those most often cited as worthy colleagues, particularly those officers from a specialist unit dealing with child abuse and who were routinely involved in child protection investigations. Child protection routines have determined more than ever before the range of acceptable agencies and related practices that practitioners now come to expect. Other agencies and their staff were now measured more by their understanding of the purpose and process of child protection activity and their facilitation of this in the way they bring issues to notice and move matters along to some stage or conclusion:

> ....the police are close to us, I think we get on pretty good with them down at the (specialist support unit) and they trust us mostly. Health are OK, though you have to watch out for some younger less experienced GPs and health visitors who refer everything. Schools are different, we see people who are child centred as on our side - and there's strong differences between the two local schools on this score, one is good one is not.

Some variation of this theme was echoed by most respondents whereby an agency's reputation tended to rest upon its grasp and support for the core project around promoting child safety via investigative and monitoring routines. But at another level the view was often shared that regardless of the effective co-operation received from agencies it was thought unlikely that most other professionals could adequately grasp what child care social work was really about:

> They still don't really know what we do - well they're not sure what we do - because it's in the philosophical and intellectual realm of interfering in other people's lives. We're simply not working on the same model as other agencies. We have to take hard decisions about children's safety and that doesn't just happen! You have to know why you are making these decisions as ethical and philosophical decisions based on children's needs and rights - not simply because of some injury or behaviour - and other professional bodies, not to mention the public, don't really understand that yet....

Perhaps this more than any other feature of contemporary welfare marked the difference between the mid 1980s and the late 1990s, that is, the dominating ethos of child centred practice where protection and safety seem now uppermost in culture and practice. Such a view was confirmed by one respondent, a qualified and experienced worker who had just joined the office:

> I read the chapter and other bits too, I can see lots of it today in the office, particularly around the way we build our own world. That was helpful to me, helped me to put into words what I was coming up against and could feel was going on. But the big difference today is that today we are assessing people really, we're into case management really, it's not called that, but that's what we do. We fulfil processes and forms, we identify needs - there's a recognition now that we can't do the hands on therapeutic stuff - even less chance if you are in the short-term team - it's wham bang. But we do try to create something of a relationship, but that's not the purpose of what we do - we're there to ensure the child is safe, then check to make sure the department is safe and if I'm safe. The children, the agency, then me. That's not cynical, that's how it works....

We now start to look more closely at 'how it works', 'it' being this small interactive world of social work where change in organisation, administration and culture have impinged more than ever before on the day to day practice of child care workers. Ten years ago the social workers in this setting enjoyed a certain degree of discretion and control over the way they worked and could negotiate to some extent what they perceived to be the intrusions of the external world, particularly that of the organisation's requirements over the completion of case records. It is towards this sphere of administrative regulation that we turn next and in doing so we will first describe how it was some ten years ago.

3   Making social work visible: official indices and false trails

This chapter will look at the formal organisational properties that operate in the setting and will display their relevance to the uncertain and unobserved practices of the child care workers. It will be shown that official indices of administrative calculation and control (written records, caseloads, case categories and case procedures) are more likely to obfuscate than reveal the way work is routinely accomplished. The occupation is of course well aware that these properties, while intended to standardise practice, are often insufficient for this purpose. However, what is absent in occupational attempts to measure or calibrate practice is an appreciation of the way workers presently substantiate their work as satisfactory or otherwise.

Within the occupation generally there is an assumption that the absence of agreed statistical criteria and clear assessment routines renders practice an ambiguous entity (see Barclay, 1982, p.24). This is not so. The social workers in the area office like others (see Satyamurti, 1981, p.58) have to manage an unpredictable work world. In doing so the child care practitioners attempt to resist external intrusion and regulate their own day to day work; in this respect practice is the outcome of a shared occupational experience. It will be shown that work is not random or unspecifiable but is assessed in highly stylised and complex supervisory relationships. It is here that members draw on their shared experiences and establish consistency and propriety of both work and worker. This occurs in a process which first denies the validity of formal administrative devices and affirms the practitioners' own methods for making unobserved practice calculable and visible. This chapter raises the former issue, that of the inadequacy and negotiability of official indices of practice. This will then clear the way for subsequent chapters to explore more fully the way workers routinely make their work visible and assessable.

It will now be shown that the socially competent member of the area office is able to apply various degrees of significance to particular official rules and artefacts. There is a 'cool alternation' (Berger and Luckmann, 1967, p.192) between the requirements of the organisation and those of the practitioner. The discrepancy between the practitioner's reality and the departmental means of official accounting and control entails subjective detachment by the experienced worker. The competent member is able both to apply and withdraw meaning for official indices in order to accomplish her daily duties.

Case categories

To begin with, each child care worker holds a caseload of varying numbers. Within each caseload individual cases are designated according to broad categories of statutory and voluntary relationships. For example, Category 'A' refers to cases that exclusively concern children who are thought to be at risk of non-accidental injury from those caring for them. Physical abuse is thus made a prime category and a separate register of children thought to be at risk of injury is also compiled. Category 'B' refers to cases where the consumer is bound by some legally instituted relationship such as various types of care or supervision orders. Category 'C' concerns cases that contain a voluntary relationship between the department and consumer in respect of child and family problems that carry no legal compulsion or duties from either party. Category 'D' addresses cases to do with the adoption and fostering of children in care of the local authority.

These categories are intended to itemise those cases that contain minimum duties in respect of visits and purpose of visiting. However, these categories give no reliable clue as to the way that workers actually manage these types of cases. Social workers readily commented that such designations were at best a very rough guide to minimum duties and that they themselves rarely relied on formal categories to construct a service. For example, it was noted that a case may be categorised as 'non-accidental injury' and thereby rank as urgent and more serious than other case types such as one requiring voluntary contact. Yet a worker may view the latter as more important due to a perceived shift in family problems. Similarly, a Category 'A' case may well have passed through a stage of crisis and the severity of the problem abated yet the designation may still remain. Likewise, a Category 'B' case such as a supervision order which is legally constructed with minimum visits and duties may be treated with less than full regard to these obligations depending on perceived priorities elsewhere in a caseload. In short, the case type gives no indication of a routine or predictable response.

Other official formulations about types of response and priority of cases exist in the departmental procedures book. Here, types of situations and relationships are encoded in broad context, for example, the book states:

First Priority Response:	Situations where adults or children are at risk of injury, disablement or death or in danger of causing this to others if intervention is not made immediately. Persons or families without immediate prospect of shelter.
Second Priority Response:	The same situations as those in first category but where feared outcome is thought less likely to be immediate.
Third Priority Response:	Investigation of referrals that do not appear to come into the first and second category. Inescapable obligations involving legal requirements, including those with time limits.
Fourth Priority Response:	Happenings in known cases which require assessment or the adjustment, re-appraisal or termination of a treatment programme.

In the procedures book there is no comment about what particular circumstances would readily fall into one 'Priority Response' or another. The procedure book guidelines are highly general and necessarily so, given the thousands of cases handled by the department. In this respect neither the procedures book or case categories provide an insight into the way workers manage their cases. In brief, social workers do not carry a set of formal responses or criteria in their heads. As the following interview extracts indicate, they have their own intimate knowledge of their own cases and this frames their reaction to various situations:

child care worker:	....you see the situation could look bad but you *know* (her emphasis) the case. You don't think - Oh! I must respond like this or this. Or, that case is now this kind of priority, er, you respond according to what you know - it's hard to say really....

39

child care worker: ....anyway my priorities are not these ones (pointing to Procedures Book), my priorities are working with cases so as to prevent these sorts of situations. You don't do our sort of work through procedures. I don't think I've even got a Procedures Book! (laughs)

Like other lower participants in occupations that deal with people's problems (see Blau, 1960, p.334; Manning, 1979a, p.57) the workers spoke of their experience of 'doing' the job as the source of their orientation towards official directives. The child care workers have learned that social work does not proceed from generalised prescriptions in categories and guidelines. They impose their own criteria on how to respond, however all agreed that suspected danger to children will receive their urgent and close attention.

This aspect of official institutional criteria stripped of significance (such as case categories and procedure responses) occurs because the multiplicity of events and contingencies in cases bears no relation to the abstract generality of broad directives. These indices or directives cannot act as a substitute for personal experience, consequently when social workers need advice they do not turn to encoded criteria but to their colleagues. The effect of this is two-fold. The worker is impelled by the insufficiency of formal directives to rely upon her own experience which she corroborates with her close colleagues. She thereby increases in-group dependence and loyalty towards local views of practice. Secondly, this insufficiency of creditable guidelines decreases collective and individual loyalty towards the organisation. This has been noted in US welfare agencies (Blau and Scott, 1963, p.235) and police organisations (Wilson, 1978, p.66). The social workers in the area office are no different. They experience the 'reality shock' of learning that the demands and dilemmas of daily work are not resolved in formal procedures nor, in the view of some, in occupational training.

new recruit in
child care team: it's not like on the course with a few cases and supervision when you want it - here you've got your own cases and you're in charge now! *You* (her emphasis) have to decide who should be seen next. And if a crisis occurs is it a

crisis? You don't get that on the course,
er the worry and the pressure. You don't
get that at college or in that (points to
procedures book).

It would seem that case categories and formal procedures have limited
relevance for the way that work is carried out and do not indicate the
amount or the style and quality of work that is applied. However, case
numbers, that is the number of cases held by a worker or by a team, does
have considerable significance as will now be shown.

Caseload numbers: '.... we've got to play it crafty....'

Each worker in the child care teams has a caseload. Within each caseload
the numbers of cases vary. The team members know that case numbers are
only a rough indication of the amount of 'work' involved with a caseload.
The fact that a worker may have far fewer cases than another team mate
does not lead to critical comments among colleagues. This is because it is
assumed that those with fewer cases may be dealing with families that
require extensive attention. These assumptions cannot be reliably tested as
there are no means of standardising the amount of 'work' a case needs. It is
left to the team leader and individual worker to estimate whether the latter
can take on more cases or has enough to do with her present caseload. This
is not peculiar to the setting in question.

The ambiguity of case numbers and the variable ways in which social
work agencies officially classify cases is a recognised occupational problem
(see Davies, 1981c, p.36). Some commentators have attributed this to the
inherent vagaries of the occupational task and the ill-defined function of
social services departments (Brewer and Lait, 1980, p.58). The disputed
significance of caseload statistics as an indication of work rate and content
(see Gould, 1981) is not a feature of social work alone. Other occupations
engaged in managing or serving the citizen rely on questionable
enumeration to justify their occupational chore. Sociologists have long
recognised that the compilation of occupational statistics can do more to
confuse than to clarify occupational processes. For example, crime rates are
a well known example of official statistics with dubious quality (see
Wilkins, 1965; Wilson, 1978, p.57; Holdaway, 1977, p130.).

The social work occupation has long been concerned with the reliability
of caseload statistics. The concern here is not to pursue this unresolved
issue but to look at the way the child care workers manage the matter. One
particular incident observed after several months of research may serve to

41

highlight the way workers view and use caseload numbers. It will be shown that case statistics are seen as important to the extent that they purport to bear witness to significant others outside the office that 'work' is being carried out satisfactorily.

The incident in question concerned a team meeting whereby members agreed to manipulate case statistics in order to secure certain team interests. This is not an activity peculiar to the team or office. All organisations contain elements that compete over scarce resources. These 'micropolitics' of organisational life give rise to alternative moral codes that legitimate the pursuit of 'local' interests (Burns, 1961, p.262). For example, the child care workers see themselves as motivated by service ideals they deem absent in their departmental hierarchy. Consequently the artful use of case statistics is not seen as some venal act but situationally justified in the circumstances (see Manning, 1977). Practitioners believe they are best placed to define the purpose and outcomes of practice. This pervasive sentiment is expressed in a linguistic tradition of gossip and rumour that bears out their lack of attachment to senior management. This tradition provides a source of 'cynical knowledge' (Goldner *et al.*, 1977) that undercuts any claim by higher members to be motivated by the same ideals as lower participants. In this way the hierarchy may, in all conscience, be stripped of moral authority in the administration of the service.

The incident in question occurred during a team meeting when child care workers and their team leader were discussing the consequences of an unfilled staff vacancy. Here their concern is that they will be expected to deal with the cases of the absent team member. The team leader allays their anxiety by stating they are going to 'play it crafty' in order that the team will not have to absorb the extra cases:

team leader:	....the applicant that was going to take Christine's place has dropped out, Pete (area office manager) has done all he can - I can say that with all sincerity, we're still trying to fill the vacancy.
Mary:	What will happen to the caseload (Christine's), will it be split? (between the team).
team leader:	No, we need it for the department, we want another worker so we need the caseload intact.

Jane:	(to team mate Sarah) But you'll be leaving in a month then we'll be two down! (turns to team leader)
team leader:	All I can say is Pete's doing his best to get someone, if anything can be done he'll do it. What I'll be doing is dragging cases around - away from some people and spreading them out a bit, some caseloads look a bit low....
Sarah:	(quickly) But numbers don't mean a thing!
team leader:	I know that - so do you - but the argument is based on numbers, if someone's got a caseload of forty-five and someone else fifteen it *looks* (her emphasis) bad. So what I want to do is a bit of redistribution. We've got to play it crafty and spread it around. After all, no one comes up and says you're doing two people's jobs - well done!
team:	(nods and murmurs of agreement)
team leader:	Basically we've closed quite a lot of Chris's cases and we could allocate the rest but we need the post (Christine's) and who knows when things blow up right? So we'll sort out the remaining cases and keep a few surplus active and add a few of your own to make it up....
Sarah:	What happens if they deteriorate?
team leader:	Well they'll all be low priority. When I was in (previous job) we kept a surplus active caseload for nine months while we had a vacancy but I'm sure they (consumers) weren't suffering. Of course it *looked* (her emphasis) bad for the department yes? But if something came up, a crisis, we gave it to someone. But we still had a caseload there! So if I'm doing strange things over the next few months you'll know why.

The team leader's plan is to allocate some of the ex-worker's cases among the team but not to the extent that the caseload will be completely absorbed. The team will take the more pressing cases and members will select from their own caseloads those cases they perceive as less of a priority. These can be added to the ex-worker's remaining caseload. This caseload will then become 'surplus active', thereby standing as evidence of an unacceptable staff vacancy. The team leader also notes that some caseloads 'look' low. The team leader, while acknowledging that case numbers are no indication of work involved, is nevertheless concerned to present a picture of caseload distributions that will prevent unwarranted scrutiny. She goes on to describe to the team that the department is now examining more closely requests for staff replacements and the appearance of caseloads with markedly different proportions might prompt enquiries into the way cases are managed.

All the team agree that the less opportunity the department has for scrutinising their local activities the better. The workers show no reluctance for this particular plan and if some of the workers have lower caseloads than their colleagues these members are not identified nor do they comment on the prospect of receiving more cases. This lack of collegial interest and comment on the relative distribution of cases in the team will be considered in the next chapter.

In view of the possibility that requests for staff replacements or staff increases will be met with close examination it is imperative that such inspection shall not pick up the wrong assumptions through an apparent imbalance in caseload statistics. Requests for more staff are considered by a number of bodies in the local authority (departmental directorate; staff review committee; social services committee; finance and personnel departments). The view of the team leader is that when caseloads 'look' roughly equal in number this will appeal to the untutored eye and ward off questions about why one worker is apparently able to deal with more cases than another. The shared belief that their occupational group might not receive a sympathetic hearing from powerful others in the local authority network means that their situation justifies the planned action.

The significance of case numbers lies in their intended use as apparent rational properties of routine practice. The appearance of caseloads that are seemingly evenly shared among members adds, in the team leader's opinion, to the appearance of orderly distributions of 'work'. Yet the team know that the number of cases in a caseload gives little insight into the way everyday work is grasped and managed. This notion of 'everyone knowing' that for all practical purposes case numbers bear scant relation to the quantity or quality of work involved, is itself an item of member-knowledge. This aspect of 'everybody knowing' the significance of numbers and their tenuous connection to 'real work' reflects processes that are characteristic of all social settings. That is, the ability of competent members to 'fill in' the unspoken assumptions that bring meaning to any account or commentary. The team members all 'know' without having to elaborate fully or explain to one another the reasons for manipulating cases and case numbers. Thus 'everyone knows' how to interpret this particular issue. They know that case numbers provide a tangible but potentially misleading dimension to work. They also know that those outside the close colleague group have no understanding or appreciation of their daily occupational experience. Consequently the workers can, with all equanimity, mislead those 'higher up' in order to make daily practice more comfortable and less amenable to outside scrutiny.

Written records: a negotiable resource

So far it has been indicated that the formal indices of administrative direction such as case categories and procedure book bear little relation to daily routine work. Instead, cases are interpreted and action taken according to the workers' view of how their cases should be prioritised and managed. Similarly, case numbers as most social workers agree are only a crude guide to the quality, type and volume of work carried out. What then of case records which are completed by social workers; do these more faithfully reflect the daily work of social workers in the area office?

To begin with, written records are a universal feature of contemporary organisations and as Weber (1948, p.197) observed, are an essential feature of the management of the 'modern office'. Records are also part of the supervisory process in modern organisations and stand as evidence of performance for supervisors and higher administrators (Blau and Scott, 1963, p.178-9). Furthermore, the writing of records and access to records by prescribed occupational members is deemed a feature of professional identity (Raffel, 1979, p.92). In the area office the importance of case histories or records is summarised in a departmental memo circulated to all workers as intended guidelines. Briefly, the document asserts that case records are an official account of work undertaken and can act as evidence of statutory obligations fulfilled by the worker. Secondly, the record is deemed an aid to practice by showing past events and changes in the pattern of relationships within the consumer's domestic setting and with the practitioner. Thirdly, records can form the basis of a management information system providing data that will inform forward planning for the department as a whole.

The departmental view is that records will serve as evidence of unobserved encounters with consumers and will provide the base for case and wider organisational planning. However, the practical activity of completing records is perceived in different ways and at different times by practitioners. As with case statistics, the workers deploy flexible assumptions that cast records as a convenient vindication of practice or, alternatively, as superfluous, time wasting and often misleading. In neither context do they view written records as an authentic source of information about their actual practices and personal competence. It would be possible at this point to add to existing comments about social work records as imperfect accounts (see Anderson, 1978; DHSS, 1981, p.21; Satyamurti, 1981, p.7) yet this would only divert attention from more important issues. These are, how are such records made sense of by practitioners and what reliance do they themselves place on these official accounts. A similar approach to the construction of health visitor records by Dingwall provides a methodological example that will be followed here:

> I am not concerned with drawing some ironic contrast between what is written in records and what 'really' goes on. The accounts inscribed on the record and the reality which they depict are integral parts of the managed accomplishment of health visiting as is the conduct of visits. (Dingwall, 1974, p.388)

In this sense records cannot simply be treated as accounts about 'work', they are also part of work itself. Writing records *is* work and one of the many skilled crafts that occur in the office. Like other workers (Goldberg and Fruin, 1976, p.12) the child care workers are largely unenthusiastic about this task and scarcely see it as a cherished mark of professional identity (see Raffel *op cit.*). In the area office records are rarely read by anyone apart from the practitioner, who typically does not view them as a relevant source of information about her own skills and practices. Instead, the records stand as a potential resource for vindicating practice in specific circumstances and do not routinely contribute to the assessment of unobserved intervention in the lives of consumers by the worker.

In the area office the manila files containing client records are kept in a central filing system. Within the files there is an array of forms and related documentation about consumers together with the written observations completed by the social worker. The records are available to managers and clerical staff who may, from time to time, require access to case details. While the case history is available to other members of the office the 'case' itself, in terms of intimate knowledge of the consumer and the service provided, is very much the 'property' of the individual worker. They refer to 'my' cases and as will be shown later there is an expectation among workers that only they are the correct arbiters of practice surrounding their caseload.

This proprietorial approach to their cases stems from the individualistic nature of the case-based task itself. The worker is responsible for her own caseload and applies her own preferred routines. Only she 'knows' about the families she visits and this privately held knowledge allows the practitioner to claim authority over the way she manages 'her' cases. This knowledge of a case, that is, the remembered incidents, experiences and hunches that a worker has about a family is largely carried in the worker's head and not recorded on files. The sheer density of detail in respect of family problems cannot possibly be fully documented and workers rely on their mental record and not the manila file for guidance in their work. While the manila files do contain accounts about practice based on this privately held knowledge they are necessarily selective and constructed in mind of the following shared assumptions and contingencies of practice:

> child care worker: I haven't waded through this lot (pointing to large manila file on desk). I got it in October (five months previous). But you see I go in where they're (clients) at - here and now - the files, er, they're background composition details - general information. I try to pick things up immediately. You try not to let the file colour you, assessments change....

As the worker indicates, case information might well become redundant over time. Furthermore, for most workers it is not simply a question of redundant information but information that is potentially refutable:

> child care worker: I personally read very little of records. I rarely go back over it. because it's often judgmental. You see it's amazing really, future generations of social workers will read my stuff and it will depend often on what I *feel*....(her emphasis)

That workers, like the one above, consider case histories to be biased in relation to the judgements or subjective opinions of previous workers does not suggest that they consider their own views to be somehow 'objective'. Instead they all acknowledge that colleagues will manage cases in the light of their own preferred styles and methods of intervention. Hence case histories are never inviolable testaments to appropriate practice. Indeed workers readily acknowledge that their style of recording and the practice it reflects will not necessarily be shared by workers who subsequently take on the case:

child care worker to researcher:	....if you look at this file you'll see that Anita (ex team member) had a terrible time with this family, look - (points to following case recording on file).
case record:	'Mr. B., has consistently refused to let me enter the house saying he can care for the children quite well 'without you lot'. I explained that I had every right to see the children as they are on supervision. He's an aggressive man with a history of drinking and was under the influence when I spoke to him. He calls me 'love' in a very sarcastic way and is probably worried that I undermine his authority in the house and his image of the 'boss' in the family. I explained that unless he co-operated I would have to go back to court as the supervision order was ineffective....'
child care worker:	You see? She had a lot of problems there. I didn't. But that's not to say Anita did a bad job - clients react differently to different workers and I get on fine with them. I don't think he's got a drink problem, but then I'm used to being with people who enjoy a drink. It doesn't upset me like it did Anita. But the bit about the 'boss' in the family, that's true, when I first went in he was very much the big man. I told him I wasn't after his

kids and he's less anxious, in fact he's a
very reasonable man once you get used
to him and get a relationship going....

This child care worker's case recording provides a distinctly different
picture of the family with the young father no longer cast as aggressive
drinker but sensitive family man:

case record: 'Mr. B., sat quietly as his wife talked
about Darren and Jenny, Mrs. B., did
most of the talking, about Darren's
truancy and the recent offence. Mr. B.,
was evidently upset saying this was the
first time Darren had been in trouble.
Mrs. B., asked him to make tea and he
returned a little later with biscuits, cups
and tray and served the tea. There
seemed little of the aggressive father I
met some weeks ago. We then discussed
the court appearance....'

The above worker, like her colleagues, can look to the record and draw
distinctions between the way the case had been handled by predecessors
and the way she wishes the case to be managed. Such differences entail no
criticism of previous workers but, on the contrary, affirm the right of each
practitioner to process her cases according to her own preferences. In brief,
two broad assumptions that govern practitioner responses to past case
histories can be discerned. First, they can eschew records as dated and
biased and thereby reinforce their own self-image of capable practitioner.
Secondly, they can respond to the records selectively in order to draw
support or confirmation for their own viewpoint:

child care worker
to team mate: Mrs. Jones has been on (telephone) again
today she won't have it that we can't
come and take her kids into care just
because they're naughty.

team mate: Yes, you've got to be a bit firm with her,
I remember the same thing with her two
years ago....

child care worker:	Um, Jackie West had the case then, there's a long history to this and she was right you know, in the file she told the mother point blank that she's got to look after them. We didn't hear any more for a few months. I'll do the same thing, I'm not having this! I can't keep running down there every time the kids play up....

Drawing inspiration and support from the record and her colleague the worker resolves to take the initiative. Yet in later months the same worker was observed to invoke the shared view that records are an insufficient source of advice and direction for present practices:

child care worker to team leader:	I've read the case notes on this one but it's not much help. Nothing's changed much in their (family) relationships and I don't think we can worry about what's happened before. It's (record) like so many cases - files with endless write-ups (written recording) but nothing in there to tell you which way to go....

As the period of observation progressed it became evident that case histories are a variable resource for the workers. For the most part they are perceived as an unsatisfying routine to be completed at the worker's convenience. Records, like other formal properties of the organisation such as rules and procedures and categories of cases, are neither binding nor explicit. Instead they are negotiated, disputed or they are conveniently brought to prominence as support for the issue at hand. This flexible use of formal properties is not a peculiarity of social work, other semi-professional and professional groups engage in similar manoeuvres (see Strauss *et al.,* 1963, p.151). In occupations such as social work where uncertain outcomes of practice are coupled with the unpredictable character of work demands, the worker has to draw on all manner of contrary resources in order to demonstrate that her activities are appropriate. Records are an instance of this. The workers do not view them as the typical means of validating their practices, rather they support, are irrelevant or indeed act as a protective barrier behind which actual practices occur. This latter aspect will now be considered. This will indicate that records, far from revealing what actually

50

occurs during intervention, can often be constructed as a gloss on what took place in order to protect the worker from unwelcome and uninvited scrutiny of her activities.

Learning to record: a question of protection

> ....now I'm sure if I write to S. he won't be living at his last address and if he did he wouldn't take any notice of the letter and I wouldn't bother him really but it's for the record. It covers us there - that's the thing - and it keeps them (higher management) happy (adding ironically) that's professional for you (laughs)....

This field note extract from an observed conversation between a social worker and a social work student introduces the negotiation of paperwork and the manner in which new members learn to structure their occupational setting to secure specific interests. The student is advised by the 'veteran' and 'learns the ropes'. She learns to manipulate records in order to bring off the appearance of expected practice. That records may be constructed for reasons of self-protection, particularly in relation to cases that may end up in court, has been briefly noted by social work educationalists (Stevenson and Parsloe, 1978, p.95). What they do not recognise is the possibility that practitioners, like others (such as policemen), who document their unobserved endeavours through records, will 'manipulate the paper reality - what the record shows - in order to achieve desired outcomes....' (Manning, 1977, p.275-6). Similarly, case records in mental hospitals may be written in purposely dense, ambiguous or irregular styles to avoid detection of sensitive details or to protect either patient or record writer (Erikson and Gilbertson, 1969; Goffman, 1968, p.144-7). The possibility that in the area office records might be written with an eye to the same interests became evident in the above extract, noted in the second month of research. However, it was not until I was well established in the setting (by some four months) that I could become a party to the following comment, made to a team leader by the worker I sat next to:

child care worker to team leader and researcher:
Look! (holding manila file) I've had this case and I've been able to do nothing with them (clients) but I've made it *look* (her emphasis) dynamic (laughs).

Well you've got to give some impression even if you can't do much - I dress it up with long words to fill the gaps, you see nothing has happened, but you have to write something....

The relevance of the extract exists not only in the fact that the worker can make an apparently discrediting remark about her own record-writing to her supervisor (a point that will be dealt with later), but also that the team leader and worker recognise the insufficiency of records as an indication of practitioner skills and the unobserved services they provide. The worker showed me the recording she had referred to and pointed to the following extract as an example of her earlier comments:

'....have visited regularly in the last three months. While relationships between Mr. and Mrs. D., have not improved there is more stability in the home and my visits have focused on the two girls. We have discussed Cathy's enuresis and sibling rivalry which I feel may be a symptom of parental conflict. This may improve if as at present there is less overt hostility between the parents. Christine is still disruptive at school but her acting out may reduce if the parents are more consistent in their control and attachment to her. I have discussed these points with the parents and will continue to monitor in fortnightly visits...'

This case recording provides a glossed summary of the worker's efforts and reveals little of her actual intentions, motivations or a more revealing account of her own activities. The record is not, therefore, a construction of past events it is a practical construction of an approved reality. For example, workers in the course of individual interviews would give examples of incidents, mistakes or sensitive matters that are best left out of official records. There was the worker who lost her temper with a family and stormed out of their house swearing at them as she left. There was the practitioner who accepted a gift from a consumer and thought it prudent to avoid recording this questionable event. Several workers stated that they knew of clients who were working when in receipt of unemployment and other state benefits. Such misdemeanours are rarely recorded or acted upon.

The writing of case histories is an acquired skill developed in the setting and reflects the contingencies and problems at hand. For example, in the instance of cases such as child abuse that might lead to a court enquiry there are lengthy detailed accounts of the practitioner's observations. The rare but dramatic legal hearings about child abuse involve a close regard for welfare records and it is generally recognised that practitioners are pressed into urgent action and high anxiety by the spectre of a child abuse case. In this respect the workers complete their records according to their interpretation of case circumstances. In the area office they write in very different styles, at varying lengths, and at their own convenience. Nonetheless, the vast majority view the exercise as a tedious but unavoidable task that gets in the way of 'real' work with the consumers. Paperwork as an obstacle to more preferred activity has been noted in other people-processing occupations such as the police force (see Walsh, 1977, p.159).

The majority of social workers describe their cases as documented in the form of summaries of varying length and detail. These provide a synopsis of their activities. A minority of practitioners state they write all records in dense detail and believe this to be a creative exercise that stimulates their ideas on the case in question. As records are rarely a source of close inspection by significant others so this influences the timetabling of their completion. A minority of workers complete their records on a weekly basis, the remainder in both child care teams inscribe their visits after two to three weeks. In a few instances months elapse before the visit is recorded. Yet all workers acknowledge the necessity to differentiate between cases that require regular and detailed recording to protect themselves and their clients:

> I spend one morning a week dictating. What I get in then I get in! But it depends on the case. If the child's heading for abuse or care I write every word, phone call, and salient point. If it's a chronic where it's a bit pointless to write it all down, it (contact with consumer) goes on and on - I write a summary....

All the workers spoke of this difference in their cases, that is, the 'chronics'. These are cases that have been 'on the books' for years, and receive periodic attention as the consumers proceed through a lengthy career of welfare involvement. It is only a minority of cases that require the special attention of elaborate recording and this is invariably in connection with cases of child abuse or children likely to be received into care.

> ....you find out what to write from your own experience, er, what you need in certain cases - potential child abuse say -

these are rare but if you go to court you've got to be sure of
your homework, er, how many times you visited, what was the
state of the property, what children were on their own, er, the
age of the baby-sitter. Er, unless you get a total picture over
time you could be in trouble with the court....

similarly:

....If there's a battering (child injury) I write fully for the child's
protection and mine. I mean I've got this fostering thing where
the parents are saying this and that (complaining about the care
of their child in a foster home) but I've got it all written down
so if we go to court and the parents say we visited every so and
so, (i.e., visited their child at the foster home on various
occasions) then I can say Oh no you didn't! Because I've got it
all written down....

   Depending on the workers' view of cases they will receive perfunctory
or highly detailed recording. In either instance the majority of practitioners
complete records more as an unavoidable routine than as a complete and
authentic reflection of their everyday activities. Like others in people-
processing occupations such as policemen (Manning, 1979b, p.267-8) and
health visitors (Dingwall, 1974, p.424-437) their knowledge of their own
work is particularistic and substantively about individual cases. The
minutiae of specific and intimate knowledge held by the workers about
their many cases can never be fully encoded in organisational records.
Instead the workers carry case records in their memories and this is the
source of reliable information that guides routine daily work. Their partial
written submissions satisfy other requirements such as a duty to record
visits to consumers bound by statutory relationships to the department.
Records are completed for protection, '....it's for the record, it covers us
there....'. Certain details will be left out altogether, or heavily emphasised
as in instances of child abuse. In these latter cases the worker will expect
her written submissions to be treated as 'facts' that may be scrutinised by a
wider audience. Contrariwise, the case history may be viewed as
contaminated by the assumptions and styles of practice adopted by previous
workers. Practitioners wish to apply their own preferred methods of
intervention and are able to deny the import of predecessors' written
comments. Written records then have their significance in the worker's
ability to derive what she wishes to discover.

It could be argued that the 'invisibility' of social work is essentially no different from other organisations where superiors rarely witness subordinates at work. Hence there is thought to be a reliance on the written reproduction of performance which is deemed essential for effective administrative control (Merton, 1957, p.342-3). However, in the area office the child care workers and their team leaders view the record as an imperfect source of information about their performance. The team leaders have practised as social workers and share this baseline experience. Like other record-writers in welfare agencies (Zimmerman, 1969) they have experienced the problems and contingencies of practice that entail the artful accomplishment of official records. All agree that records are potentially impressionistic and bear witness to the preferred assumptions and methods of practice of themselves and their predecessors. They also recognise that records are intended and constructed as 'fact'; indeed it is a mark of the experienced member that she can interpret or complete records to manage these contrary assumptions surrounding case histories.

While workers and supervisors recognise that records are an insufficient indication of practitioner competence, the record nevertheless stands as a form of evaluation in relation to specific team members. Records become a form of supervisory control at particular moments in the careers of new or recently trained recruits. Recruits are an unknown quantity during their initial months at the office and the supervisor has to gradually acquire some idea of the newcomer's range of abilities and experience. This cannot be achieved by some direct oral examination or interrogatory routines of direct questioning. This would offend the shared notion that all are qualified and capable practitioners. Instead the supervisor looks to the case record as a means of managing a delicate interactive event. The record stands as a conductor between both parties whereby they can appeal to it to display their respective concerns and interests. This bears similarity to Blau and Scott's (1963, p.178-9) observation of statistical performance records in a public employment agency. Here the supervisor points to numerical data rather than baldly asserting her own opinion of the subordinate. By appealing to the record the supervisor can transform her comments into offers of support or advice rather than criticism, after all, the record 'speaks' for itself. This very point is made by a team leader in the office setting:

> I don't have time to read records that much, the cases come
> through to me on their way back from the typists and I usually

give them straight back to the team. I might glance at ones that are causing a bit of worry - like Karen's cases, the cases aren't so bad but Karen's only been with us a few weeks so I just keep a check on her files. It gives you an idea of what she's doing, how she sees things. What I do is keep a couple of her cases to one side, there's a dodgy one there and we go over it in supervision. It helps you to think about the client and what she's doing with them....

In further interviews with the team leaders it was possible to explore this aspect of the new recruit. From these discussions it was clear that the supervisors use the record to probe and examine the new worker's skills and attachment to certain service ideals. As in other neophyte-supervision situations (see Ditton, 1977, p.29) the supervisor wishes to be sure the newcomer believes in the shared rationale of the occupational group and does not simply act out or reluctantly conform to these ideals. In the setting the supervisor assesses this requirement in a studied replay of the new worker's practice. To do this she uses the record to probe the recruit's unobserved activities and attitudes. The record contains a source of topics and issues and by referring to these the supervisor can raise and frame questions that might otherwise appear overly intrusive. However, as the team leader becomes more acquainted with the new member and creates a developing rapport she can supervise without recourse to the record. The supervisor has thus 'learned' about the worker and can assess her suitability, skills and conduct, without relying on the record. She can now question and discuss within the comfort of an established collegial relationship.

Once the new member is 'known' the record is no longer prominent and it reverts to its typical location of lesser and desultory occupational task. Over time a process of familiarisation has occurred whereby organisational knowledge in the form of the record has been displaced by knowledge of the person who constructs the record. This aspect of records and the assessment of performance has been suggested in Raffel's (1979, p.85-9) analysis of bureaucratic evaluation. He notes that the absence of observers to a particular performance entails dependence upon other routines for assessing the reliability of conduct. Such dependence does not necessarily entail a vigorous testing of written documents but may instead be an issue of whether the recorder in person can be relied upon.

In the context of the area office the team leaders 'witness' the unobserved encounter with consumers through their accumulating knowledge of the practitioner. Thus, if records are poorly constructed or incomplete this does not indicate the quality of performance. This has been assessed and continues to be grasped in the supervisory relationship whereby member and team leader learn more about the interests and abilities of each other. Like those who deal with personal services to patients and clients (see Roth, 1964, p.300-1) the members rely upon observation and information that is passed by word of mouth and collects into an oral history of both the practitioner and her cases. This was confirmed when discussing the issues of case recording with a recent child care recruit. She had been a member of the office for several months when interviewed, and was now established in the setting and the team. During the interview she includes the following comment which indicates her change of attitude towards records and her change of status in the office. She is no longer an unknown quantity - she is 'known' :

.... I'm very bad with recording, I do summaries - suddenly it's July, September, October! (laughs) I mean some of the cases I've got if you were doing it (recording) every week there'd be a screed like this (raises arm above desk). You only need a summary. As long as I know I'm putting the work into it and I think my team leader knows and my area officer knows I'm putting the work into it, er, in fact I've just done a summary of *four months* (her emphasis). But I don't feel guilty - they *know* (her emphasis) I'm putting a weekly input into the cases....to begin with when you first come you tend to justify the work you're doing, er, in May and June I did good recording - recording every visit! (laughs) But now I don't feel I have to justify the work I do because they *know* (her emphasis) what I'm like....

The recruit is now 'known', how she is 'known' and through what processes and criteria will be the general topic of the next two chapters. The point here is that the social workers learn that records are not routinely intended to provide authentic sources of information about their own skills and abilities. Instead written records like case categories, case statistics and official procedures, are shifting relevances in a complex occupational world. These formal organisational features may be discounted, ignored or indeed applied with full vigour, and it is the socially competent member of the setting who can adroitly negotiate the contrary and incompatible assumptions that surround official artefacts. The practitioners can do so with some equanimity for they know that their unobserved performance with consumers is understood and shared in contexts very different to those discussed so far and where assumptions differ significantly from those contained within official criteria.

Ten years later

A decade later there seemed to have been relatively little change in much of what has just been described. For example, there was no weighting system used to appraise case complexity and guide the distribution of work other than the team manager's view of what demands a case might make on the worker in question. New cases were given directly by team managers to individual workers, allocation at team meetings was no longer the mode, hence team members were even less likely than before to know what cases a colleague might have:

> I've no idea what cases come up and who has what - I still think some sort of weighting system would be fairer and safer but we have never gone down that road....

A decade before there had been some fourteen full time qualified workers dealing with just over 600 active cases. Ten years later there was the same number of qualified staff in both teams but additionally there were ten unqualified workers employed as family carers or social work assistants, dealing in all with just under 550 active cases. Most qualified practitioners had around twenty to twenty five active cases and unqualified staff tended to have more on the assumption that they would deal with less problematic work. This difference from before was keenly noted by one long serving worker:

> When I was first here in the late 1980s we had ridiculous number of cases, we'd have a caseload of over fifty, loads of kids in care and constant reviews. A lot of that has gone, now we have caseloads in their twenties, we're into family support when there's time, but generally it's children at some sort of risk. We're more focused than before, clear about why we're there....

For qualified staff, caseloads were now smaller, more intensive and more closely drawn around families where there was significant concern over the safety or well-being of a child. Social work assistants and family carers engaged more in family support work and had larger caseloads than their qualified colleagues. As before, staff generally tended to treat the case record as a negotiable resource, particularly those past events depicted by any previous practitioner who had worked on the case; such views could generally be cast as confirmatory or irrelevant to current practice. Thus for some staff, a new case with a past record of involvement with the office was not always seen as a useful source of information likely to yield valuable insights into family history:

> You could plough through this (points to record) for days and still not really get to know that family - who would have an entirely different view to this anyway - I'm not wasting too much time on it (record). I'll make my own mind up when I've been out to see them a few times....

As before, the workers saw paperwork as a burden and most alluded in some way to the encroachment this made upon their direct work with clients. Yet, here certain differences began to emerge between the assumptions and activities of a generation ago and their successors, particularly in relation to record keeping as 'real work'. A decade ago, paperwork was seen as peripheral to the central project of child care, ten years later there had been a significant change. It was not that completing records and other allied documentation were in any way more popular, far from it, but that it was now seen as a major plank of practice and one that, in their view, demanded diligence and reliability:

> I hate the bureaucratic stuff, but I'm good at it though, you have to be, there's reports not just for here but for court, for reviews, planning meetings, you name it. Recording is key to what we do, the job has changed from your chapter. You see, with child protection, people have to be confident in what you say, and that you will do what you say - the written word is taken much more seriously than when I first did social work....

This worker described how a range of significant others would now read the various written productions that practitioners might have to submit for formal scrutiny. That this was now a customary feature of practice as were the various meetings at which such documentation were studied, was frequently cited by respondents. Likewise, they insisted that 'outsiders' were unlikely to appreciate the extent to which social workers were now engaged in administrative processes that could never have been anticipated even a few years ago, and for which they felt unprepared by their social work training:

> We write for case records, for statutory reviews, for core group meetings, for other agencies, for court, you name it - it's relentless - but you have to do it in this line of work - it's protection stuff, it's for the child and for you. You need to always be able to show that visits have been made, that decisions have been taken and who's taken them. You cover your back this way. Now we never got that side of it in training, you still don't learn enough in training about how to recognise risks and express these in such a way that you are stating fact and not gossip or wishful thinking, you know, on paper and in front of people, that's a skill today. That's where we differ from them in your chapter - that seemed alien to me, you know, the highly descriptive stuff about families - the colour and background, all that creative stuff! We don't do that anymore, it's now about risks, decisions, control. It's not about a relationship so much - that is there of course but it's about getting the facts across - we can only operate on facts. The court will want facts - they'll want to know about a child's wishes of course but it's all about what happened and what can be done about it....

It would be wrong to assume that all cases are written up with the same detail and single-mindedness as claimed in the above extracts. These after all were qualified workers dealing mainly if not exclusively with child protection cases. Other workers, such as the family carers and social work assistants were generally less involved in such cases and described a more relaxed approach to record keeping unless some crisis or key decision arose. Yet, the above extracts mark out the dominant ethos around paperwork. It was no longer a gloss on 'real work' but was itself part of practice that the competent worker would complete with a careful eye to the various possible readerships, not all of whom could be counted upon as sympathetic to the worker's aims.

Such a perspective was strongly reinforced by the two team managers in the office who clearly and intentionally set the tone for this sphere of work. Both team managers had read the chapter and recognised many of the continuities over the ten year period that the workers had noted above. Where they did depart decisively from their predecessors was over their insistence that careful construction of written material was a core part of the professional repertoire and a major indicator of the 'good' worker. However, records by themselves did not usually stand as sufficient evidence of practitioner competence. Team managers did not have time to check all records and during supervision they would only have time to discuss the more pressing cases in any detail. Thus they would typically rely on the worker's oral account and their own notes from previous supervision sessions about what action had been decided upon in order to measure both case and practitioner progress in line with their assumptions of 'good work'. The essential concern for these team managers, as for practitioners, was written material as a record of 'facts' and the dutiful completion of such records as a hedge against what was widely perceived as a blame culture in which child protection workers had to operate:

> ....well we don't write like they did in your book anymore. Speculation is not on. You have to be able to support any theory you may have. You can't write 'I think they may have done this or that'. You avoid that stuff. People will write up records in case they have to make a statement for a care order. They will write with a beginning, middle and end, a sequence of events. None of the vague stuff they used to write that you describe - they stick to the facts er... for planning meetings, placement meetings, core group, stat' reviews. They go to endless meetings and they need to know what they're going there for and what they want - so they have to have the facts with them....

While team leaders did not have time to read case records or monitor their completion in some systematic manner they did maintain a watchful eye on the cases that were likely to be troublesome and would seek assurances from staff that work was properly written up. They did so because of their own concern over exposure to criticism in what they perceived to be an occupational world with many potential pitfalls. For example, clients, unlike before, were now routinely invited to meetings where they could if they so wished, challenge the description of events surrounding their case and related decisions. Clients now had greater access to records, to complaints procedures, to elected members. Similarly, the public, which provided many confidential or anonymous tip-offs, were the source of the largest number of referrals over child abuse after health and the police. In such a context, the team leader could in her mind's eye imagine some indignant client or disappointed informant contacting the media and could easily anticipate the swift response of senior managers and local councillors to any pointed questions from newspapers or TV journalists:

> Today there is more emphasis upon watching your back especially with that (names ongoing enquiry into alleged dereliction of duty by social work manager in neighbouring authority) going on - what a nightmare - it could happen to any of us in this business. If the press or TV get a story then you have councillors and management all over you, and not in some protective sense, they want answers that prove we did it right. Your head's on the block if you haven't done it right. So I do it by the book, we record what happened, and in supervision I check that they are keeping the files up to date on certain cases. I will have my agenda as well, I will have notes on our last supervision and I will want to see what's been happening since to those cases. I can't go through every case, so I rely on them to bring up the ones they are worried about as well as the ones I'm interested in.

This viewpoint was shared by both team leaders who, like many of their staff, believed that 'blame' was now an inevitable if occasional feature of doing social work. This was not simply because of the enthusiasm with which the media might run a story but because staff believed in an open and participatory association with users who would as a matter of good practice be notified of avenues for raising grievances. Given the highly charged nature of the work, complaints came to be seen as a probable hazard to be prepared for rather than viewed as an unexpected threat from without. Complaints had increased in recent years and were described by staff as taken seriously by management and dealt with rapidly. Indeed, staff were generally of the view that managers appeared to accept complaints at face value until convinced otherwise (or not) by social workers or team managers:

> It's still like it was in the chapter but its just more intense now, there's great pressure on not getting it wrong. A greater sense of insecurity, er investigation, the fear factor is almost tangible - there but for the grace of God. Ten years ago we were looser, perhaps more vague, simply didn't know so much. Today the expectation is different. We're vulnerable to much more criticism and criminal charges as you can see from (names investigation in neighbouring authority). So, everyone is into a

blame thing. If there's a complaint they (senior management) assume that there is substance to it and the attitude is one of 'well how do you explain this then?'. And I don't think we feel very protected in this work against unfair comments from clients. It's almost as if they (senior management) immediately take the side of the complainant. So, I write everything down, I record the decisions I have made in supervision with the team manager, so that it's not just my neck it all lands on....

The climate of anxiety around 'getting it wrong' in child protection is perhaps the most dramatic change that has occurred over the last decade. It is now a compelling feature of not simply the psychology of practice as 'dangerous work' but is also a prominent element of administrative control in that workers are now more closely monitored by supervisors than before, as we shall see in later chapters. Thus, if the balance of statutory child care has moved to a more forensic and surveillance oriented activity then so too has the role of supervisor, and here the record can play a key part in the team manager's careful scrutiny of practice. For example, while team managers cannot read every case they nonetheless impress upon workers the imperative of routine recording, a point well described by one team manager:

Today, you need closer attention to events in order to detect patterns around what's going on in a case or in the family. Weeks can fly by and you can't assume a worker will always be visiting as they should, or if they are that they are writing it up. But now we have a form they have to clip to the front of the case which shows at a glance what visits have happened. If there are care proceedings you must write up quickly after a visit to get recall OK, or you will be challenged in court. So now we have a grid that shows dates of visits and the top of the grids has columns with child protection register, core group meeting, statutory review, statutory visit, family support visit. and you have an idea when these should happen - you know x number of weeks - and so you can see if all the checks are being done....

This shift to a more self protective and 'fact' based approach to recording and monitoring work was far removed from over a decade before. Accompanying this was a much clearer structure for the coding of referrals and cases and their contents than ever before. There were now clear procedures to be followed within specified time periods in respect of different types of referral, notably those requiring a child protection investigation or where there was serious concern over a child's welfare. These two types of referral comprised the vast majority of issues that were accepted by child care staff who worked on reception. The department's very clear requirements and procedures over documentation were encoded for all workers in departmental guidelines based in part on Children Act (1989) guidance and regulations. Within the guidelines there existed minimum case recording standards to be achieved in respect of child care plans, children on the child protection register, statutory visits and reviews, family support cases, disclosure of cases, monitoring of cases and filing, transfer and closure of cases. The detailed nature of these procedures bore little resemblance to the way cases were written up, used and interpreted by staff and managers of a decade ago. As one team manager said:

> Your chapter said that records were not seen as 'real work'.
> Well they are now. Real work is doing reports well, there's no
> room for vagueness anymore. Our cases are categorised
> according to whether children are 'being looked after', on the
> child protection register, or getting family support services, and
> the way files are structured is much more clear - this is not
> about Admin taking over control, it's about sound professional
> work, this *is* (speaker's emphasis) social work....

It was made clear by both team managers that, unlike before, diligent recording in line with prescribed criteria was itself an important element of professional practice. Yet, it was also acknowledged that records alone were not the sole basis by which work was assessed as satisfactory or otherwise. As noted above, team managers had time only to read a small number of selected records. For the most part they were more concerned to establish if records were being kept up to date in respect of key events and here they relied on a mixture of their knowledge of the worker, the worker's comments, and the completion by staff of a form fastened to the front of a case, indicating meetings held and visits made. From these sources they were able to assess if work was progressing satisfactorily towards agreed aims. It is this realm of what constitutes satisfactory work that now comes to prominence. It will be shown that the changes noted here are not just matters of administrative routine but of worker control as well. Some new and very different relationships had grown between team colleagues and between staff and managers as the next two chapters will illustrate. It will be seen that there are many continuities from ten years before but some profound differences as well which now permeate the way 'good work' and 'good workers' are made visible and understood within the setting. First we look at colleague relationships as they were a decade or so ago.

4 Issues of visibility and colleague relationships

The child care workers occupy a negotiable occupational world wherein situations call forth contrary and variable definitions. For example, the workers deftly apply and withdraw moral affect from the procedures and documentation that officially detail practice. These formal requirements of the organisation are managed through tacit and unwritten understandings that are acquired by the competent member of the office setting. Through these understandings the members defend themselves against what they perceive to be an unsympathetic work environment. They preserve their cherished sense of self-regulation and preferred ways of managing their cases and like other small groups in large organisations (Roy, 1952; 1953; 1960), they seek to control the pace of their activities. Their individual and collective resistance to intrusion entails shared assumptions about practice and the assessment of work. It is precisely this aspect of the setting that now comes to prominence.

The evaluation of work: the practitioners' viewpoint

The evaluation of social work has taxed the occupational imagination and the issue has fuelled criticisms of welfare claims to beneficial intervention (see Geismar, 1972, p.31; Lait, 1980, p.49). Occupational literature in America and Britain recognises the substantial problems of reliably assessing the impact of practice. The pessimistic results of much research into welfare effectiveness are well known to educationalists and occupational representatives. Their response to research critical of social work practice falls into three broad categories. First, there is the view that the structural problems (poverty, class inequalities) that frequently arrive at social work agencies resist amelioration by welfare alone (Meyer, 1973, p.94; Wasserman, 1975, p.184-195; Olsen, 1980, p.3). Secondly, there is the assertion that much research to date fails to appreciate fully the complexity and subtlety of welfare relationships and that conventional research methods fail to capture the nuance of welfare intervention (see Herstein, 1969; MacDonald, 1966, p.189; Irvine, 1969; Plowman, 1969; Robinson, 1971; Rose, 1957). A third response has been to recognise the hazy nature of much welfare activity and to then exhort practitioners to demonstrate through more rigorous practices that intervention has been and can be successful (see Sheldon, 1978, p.2; 1981; Hardy, 1970; Baird, 1981a; Goldberg and Fruin, 1976, p.6).

In this continuing debate about social work's effectiveness there is a tendency to ignore the question of how work is routinely accomplished at present. There is all too often the assumption that work is somehow inchoate and unspecifiable. Yet this clearly neglects the way that practitioners presently construct a meaningful work setting that, for all intents and purposes, makes practice an orderly and creditable endeavour. Consequently, the workers will not be viewed here as the imperfect denizens of an unstructured work-world deviating from proper practice. Rather, the daily setting will be revealed as the authentic and purposeful construction of members who competently employ their own assumptions and 'theories' of what constitutes good work.

Like all of us, social workers have their common-sense theories about their daily sociation. Like others in occupations that manage people and problems they do not match their efforts to the 'Book'; be it the formal theories of practice or the official regulations of the organisation. Instead they draw on their shared occupational experiences and beliefs to substantiate and accomplish practice. Thus, probation officers cannot predict a successful outcome to their interventions, rather they believe their efforts to be intrinsically worthwhile (Davies, 1972; Raynor, 1978). Policemen do not always police according to official procedures but invoke their own notions of good practice and means for assessing this (Manning, 1977, p.269; Walsh, 1977, p.155-159). Teachers operate beyond the scrutiny of an external audience and often pursue what they think constitutes successful classroom activity (Bishop, 1977). In brief, other occupations apart from social work operate in an uncertain work environment and often without clear criteria of what is successful or unsuccessful practice. The concern here therefore is not what constitutes welfare effectiveness but rather how do workers themselves make sense of their occupational uncertainties.

'....you can 't see a lot of progress in this job and I don't see any point in looking for it....' everyday evaluation in the area office

Observation and interview data gathered from the child care teams suggested that it is the misguided researcher, rather than the workers, who tries to glean some definitive notion about occupational practices and outcomes. Workers know from 'doing' the job that social work does not fall into a sequence of acts that can be categorised, enumerated or unpacked for those 'outside' to simply see and appreciate. Instead work is the learned skill of juggling competing demands and responding to unwelcome emergencies. Work also includes the lulls between urgent demands and the discretionary use that can then be made of time. Social work is not a monotonous series of identical activities but essentially the varied practices of workers who largely regulate their own daily efforts.

All the child care workers have to share in the experience of uncertainty about their intervention in the lives of children, parents and families. Like other social workers (Mattinson and Sinclair, 1980, p.294) they rarely speak of 'cures' or 'success' but assume their intervention to be beneficial. Notions of success or failure are displaced by an emphasis upon the necessary and worthwhile quality of the service they provide irrespective of outcome:

child care worker: I have four girls who went into care -that
                       hit me - I wasted four years on them. But
                       then it's not a waste - it's caring and that
                       means something. But I know you can't
                       see a lot of progress in this job and I
                       don't see any point in looking for it....

child care worker: One thing you can't do - you can't
                       measure care. But you see the work *is*
                       caring (her emphasis). I think it's the
                       caring aspect, it sounds a bit slushy and
                       that - but it's there. You know it's
                       working in there even if you don't see
                       results....

Like other workers (see Sainsbury, 1975, p.106-7) the child care practitioners hold varying views about the impact of their actual practices. Some assume their efforts are always beneficial, irrespective of outcome. Others believe their efforts will have little influence but persist in the hope of future beneficial outcomes. The 'good' worker carries on despite demoralising results:

> child care worker: ....I mean with Derek, I was thinking two and a half years I've been working with him! What have I done? (he had just been received into care for offending). I can't come to grips with it sometimes. So I don't know how you monitor progress, you can never really weigh whether it's your intervention or the milkman's! OK, Derek would have been in care perhaps twenty times more than he was, had I not been there - but I really don't know. You just sort of go on....

This uncertainty of practice does not become a hindrance to the processing of cases. Workers carry on. They visit clients, attend meetings, complete documents and records, contact other agencies and secure resources where they can for their clients. Their day to day routines and competing demands stand as implicit testimony to the assumption that their efforts are necessary and rational.

Thus, while the child care workers may admit their uncertainties, they nevertheless persist; they push their doubts to one side and respond to the demands of the day. This is aptly illustrated in the following extract. Here a worker describes her anxieties over a case where a child has been received into care. Receptions into care, as she states, are not an indication of some failure on her part. She is not going to concern herself with any demoralising question about possible shortcomings in her previous work with the family or alternative strategies that might have prevented the child's removal from home. Instead she responds to the immediate task and ensures that each stage of the child's removal is planned and properly executed. As she states, she can devise a 'strategy' for the present problem. Whether this is the 'correct' strategy or the outcome of faulty prior intervention are questions that resist easy answers:

> child care worker: ...er I'll tell you what it doesn't do, it doesn't do, er, to look back on your cases and wonder was that successful? 'Cos if you do that (pauses) let me give you an example, er, taking David into care. As

69

far as I'm concerned I'm taking each step at a time and each step was the right one to take - you know - we tried everything. But! If we go back to the beginning and say should that child *ever* (her emphasis) have been allowed to come into care and if I had made more efforts with the family earlier would he have been in care today? I mean I'm happy with each successive stage but if I go back, was there the right decision at the beginning? You see I can be successful in my strategy but whether that was the right strategy I don't know. I must forget that - if I worry about that I'll never get anywhere! Particularly when you take children into care....

Here the worker emphasises her attention to a well-conceived plan of how to manage the various stages of receiving a child into care (where to stay, for how long, who may visit and so forth). This distinction between a competent handling of the case and wider issues of being 'right' or 'successful' has been noted about the professions generally (see Hughes, 1958, p.96). For example, while the lay person may view success in social work as 'solving' the individual or family problem, the practitioner may be more concerned with following legal procedures or completing records and applying specific resources or routines. The relevance of Hughes' comment lies in this distinction between a 'competent' and a 'successful' handling of a problem. The professional, in this instance the social worker, manages the problem in a proper and competent way: whether this is undeniably the 'right' course of action is an issue she must not worry about unduly.

Uncertainties and anxieties are components of the social work experience. There are few reassuring aspects of practice. There are unanticipated breakdowns in family relations, furthermore, family stability cannot be easily attributed to the workers' specific efforts. Assumptions of beneficial or necessary intervention displace doubts about the efficacy of service. Unending demands on workers' time have to be met and practitioners apply themselves to the exigencies of the moment.

The social workers manage their own cases and have no formal routines for investigating the case practices of their team mates. Occupational uncertainties are experienced in this entrepreneurial mode of practice.

However, the anxieties are to some extent resolved in shared assumptions about the necessity and propriety of their collective endeavours. It is towards this partially shared and partially private world of team membership that the enquiry moves. For the matter of team membership has a profound impact on the way that child care work is shared and made visible in the office setting.

Shared assumptions and private practice: the social work team

Large elements of the child care workers' organisational lives are undefined by formal procedures or precise criteria. It is left to the individual and the group to structure a world that resolves occupational uncertainties. This is managed through the communication of problems, aspirations, fears, myths and so forth that construct shared reference points that validate and chart the workers' activities and progress. Like organisational participants elsewhere (Hughes, 1968, p.20; Roth, 1968, p.25-40) the social workers create their own sense of career location and esteem within the daily collegial group. The child care workers do not look out to a clearly marked career future. In many respects they have 'arrived'. They are qualified and assert their own tasks as the core elements of the occupational endeavour. They create their own subjective dimension of career and their place in the organisation. Their lack of affection for the organisational hierarchy denies managerial locations as a fit ambition for practitioners. Instead promotion out of the 'field' is seen as an undignified escape route for those who cannot cope with the rigours of 'real' work with consumers.

Thus it is no failure to stay a social worker while other contemporaries may have advanced to higher positions. Both new and veteran workers build up conceptions of honour and prestige and like other workers who remain in the same location for long periods (Becker and Strauss, 1968, p.28) they assert the importance of their task - only they are doing the 'real' work. Thus the workers emphasise to all concerned that they are self-regulating capable practitioners. In order to sustain this shared self-conception collegial relationships are carefully managed in the following ways.

The child care workers typically know little of the cases held by their team colleagues or the preferred skills they apply to these cases. It could be assumed therefore that this 'pluralistic ignorance' leads to unfounded assumptions about the spread of shared attitudes and practices among the team (see Merton, 1968, p.431). While this occurs to some extent it does not preclude coherent and predictable team relationships. In the course of interviews it became apparent that workers have very different caseloads that are oriented towards certain types of consumers. This was not based on a 'formal' decision to specialise or major in certain types of problems. Rather this has evolved as practitioners have displayed interests and skills in some areas rather than others. For other workers it was simply a question of the way a caseload had developed and changed over time and there was no conscious decision to practice in a particular area of work:

> I'm mostly involved with youngsters coming before the court, but I do some fostering and adoption....

> Um, the majority of my work I would describe as crisis work with families. Very little in the way of preventive work....

> We get, er, well I get a lot of mentally ill mothers....

> I seem to be dealing with adolescents mainly, but its just happened that way, but in a few months new cases could all be different....

Briefly, the workers have very different caseloads and manage these in the light of their own preferred methods of intervention. The possibility that this entrepreneurial style of practice could lead to variation in the quality of service has been noted elsewhere (see Stevenson and Parsloe, 1978, p.328). Yet this variation in caseload contents and practice rarely becomes a topic of interest for team members. Typically they know little about colleagues' cases apart from 'notorious' consumers whose names are commonly known:

> You hear about some clients but generally we get on with our own cases. In fact I wouldn't know how my cases compare with others - I suppose they're similar....

> ....I think the demands made on us are different. Er, I do more adolescent girls. Well that's my impression....

Within the office there are no official routines that provide the workers with an opportunity to compare cases, case numbers or methods of practice. Like other social workers (see Stevenson and Parsloe, 1978, p.77-8) they are more concerned to get on with their own cases than to take a close interest in colleagues' practices. Nevertheless, team members slowly accumulate clues and insights into the way other workers manage their caseloads:

....it's something we don't talk about. The names (consumers) come out that trouble everyone, but as far as a caseload goes and what they (team mates) do, I wouldn't know. (Probe). Er, I know Joan gets home early most days for her boy from school. I know Michelle has a lot of evening visits because of adolescents and Jean to my mind works far too hard! I'll say to Jean are you going home now and she'll say 'No, I'm off to East Town' and this is five o'clock! Basically you get to know how they work over the years....

Social work, as I was regularly reminded by practitioners, is really learned on the job. So too are collegial relationships. As the interview extract below indicates, there is a process of learning about colleagues. That is, time experience and observation provide the practitioner with some understanding of how team mates operate. In this instance a new recruit to the office refers to this process of accumulating clues about her team mates:

Here (area office) the atmosphere is different, it's supportive and you can cope with a caseload, but I've no idea how many cases they've got. They don't moan about evening work and take time off if they need it. Er, I'm still sussing it out really....

It will now be demonstrated that in the office the team member demonstrates her competence not by reference to formal social work methods or theory but to the shared assumptions that surround collegial relationships. This is not to suggest that formal theory and methods have no bearing but that in routine team interaction such knowledge is rarely raised in conversation or meetings. Like other social workers (Stevenson and Parsloe, 1979, p.134-5) the team members do not usually describe their activities in formal theoretical contexts. Whether such knowledge is being applied is not the methodological issue here. Rather it is the question of what makes a worker a competent member of the setting. In this sense it is not social work theory or methods that make the good worker, instead it is as Becker (1972, p.98) observes, the 'on the job' learning of the obligations and rights of everyday membership that shapes practice and occupational identity. It will now be shown that a competent member of the team learns the prevailing mores of colleague relationships. It will be shown that these entail an aversion to tests of comparative ability among team mates and an emphasis upon a skilful blend of collegial support and individual autonomy. Learning this is a crucial mark of the 'good' worker.

Minimal scrutiny - maximum harmony: lessons in colleagueship

Throughout the research it was apparent that individual differences of caseload and styles of practice did not lead to division or competition among team mates. This stems from the workers' tacit understanding that all are capable practitioners. To enquire or comment on another's work intrusively would offend this arrangement. Like other professionals (see Strauss et al 1964, p.311) the team mates negotiate an interactive order that promotes a comfortable harmony and precludes an uncomfortable scrutiny of collegial practice. This order does not simply exist but is daily constituted within the team. Over time members learn the persisting convention surrounding cases. That is, the case and caseload constitute a bailiwick for the individual worker.

The practitioners expect support for, or at least polite acceptance of, their styles of practice. During the course of research only one heated debate occurred about the management of a case. This took place when a case was being allocated to a worker during a team meeting (case allocation will be discussed in chapter five). It is significant that disagreement occurs at this time, that is, when the case is not the established preserve of a specific worker. In the extract below it can be seen that once the case is finally allocated discussion ceases and conversation moves on to the next case. The case in question concerns a young boy who has not attended school for some weeks. Contrary opinions are expressed that suggest the problem lies with the family, or, with the family and school. In the course of this disagreement one of the workers volunteers to take the case saying:

child care worker:	I've heard of this family from some of my clients in the same street and I don't think it's the school. There's a lot of problems with the father and I don't think the boy wants to go to school and dad encourages him.
team mate:	OK. You say the lad won't go to school but I'm saying I know the school and there's a lot wrong with it. I don't think much of the way they handle kids with problems but anyway it's up to you.

74

| child care worker: | Yes, I take your point but I've got my own thoughts on this one (puts case into briefcase and snaps it shut firmly and looks to the team leader). |
| team leader: | Right. Let's move on. We've got another one (case) from Arabella Street, the GP's referred mum because.... |

The disagreement comes to a close as the worker firmly shuts her briefcase and thereby clearly signals the end of discussion. The team leader takes the cue and swiftly moves on to allocating the next case without taking part in any of the discussion. The team leader, like the practitioners, subscribes to the view that workers are capable, self-directed practitioners and if she is concerned about any aspects of worker-performance then the team meeting is not the place to take this up. Workers likewise support the notion that critical scrutiny of another's case offends the studied consensus of team relations, a point well put by one team member to the researcher:

| child care worker: | ....there's a strong tendency that any critical analysis of what you're doing, er, would mean criticism of perhaps a colleague and we don't do it. We sort of play the happy family.... |

The 'happy family' is the negotiated and carefully managed appearance of team harmony. Observation and interview material document a persisting view of the team as a comfortable resource for advice and understanding. Surrounded by an uncomfortable and sometimes hostile world the team provides a safe haven. Like other occupations unsure about their popular recognition, such as the police (Walsh, 1977, p.153) the social workers look to themselves for the affirmation they deem absent elsewhere. In this respect the team resembles a 'clique', that is, a collusive group which maintains a sense of worth and rational purpose in the face of an unsympathetic environment. As Burns (1955, p.474) suggests, the clique is a defensive formation characterised by its members' critical disavowal of other groups or elements in the organisational network. Within the clique the members engage in gossip, jokes and a cynical view of their occupational arrangements. This acts as a form of social control on those 'outside' and marks out the 'insiders' of this intimate gathering.

Within the child care teams there are observable patterns of interaction that indicate selective relationships. Here members seek more private confidences and support and thereby choose specific colleagues for this purpose. This was confirmed during interviews when eight of the fourteen workers described how they were prepared to find time for particular colleagues, but could not extend themselves to all the team. Their comments indicated regular advice-sharing among three pairs of workers. Also, within these pairs two of the participants sought out, to a lesser extent, the opinions and support of another team member. Like other workers (Blau 1964, p.36) these team members engage in informal but regular consultancy partnerships. They are typically the more recently qualified members and with less than four years of experience. Four veterans within the two teams who have much more than four years experience are notably independent of partnerships. Two recent recruits still consult all who have the time or inclination to respond.

The giving of advice exists in all organisations but it is rarely a purely voluntary or 'politically innocent' event (Bryson, 1952, p.203). People base advice-giving and receiving on certain status expectations and reciprocities. For example, all the team members were reluctant to approach their team leaders too often for advice as this might indicate over-dependence and hence questionable competence. Instead most workers who engage in consultancy relationships construct partnerships that entail no subordination of status. Participants draw on shared assumptions of complementary skills and abilities. Interview data suggests that workers seek the support of a colleague whose skills and attitudes are similar to their own and they avoid those who they consider might advance assertively their own viewpoint:

> Anita (veteran) is a bit er how can I put it. She's really nice but she'll take over if you let her. She's a good friend of mine, she's a good worker, but her ways aren't my ways. I don't talk to her about my cases....I generally talk to Suzanne, she tells you what she thinks and leaves it there.

While several of the workers do engage in partnership advice-giving they do of course talk to other members of their team and exchange ad hoc comments on matters of the moment. For example, a worker might talk out loud without aiming her remarks at anyone in particular. This may be described as 'consultation in disguise' (Blau, 1964, p.35), here the speaker hopes that her remarks may be taken up and pursued by colleagues if they have the time. Alternatively, team mates may nod sympathetically or simply ignore the tacit offer to stop and talk shop:

> ....you can spend all day talking about cases if you're not careful! I talk to Yvonne (team mate) if I'm really worried about a case and she lets me know about her bad ones. We started here about the same time so we sort of grew up together if you like. She talks to me or Melanie. But I keep my head down most of the time, otherwise you'd get nothing done!

Despite the selectivity of advice-seeking and the evident disparity of practices and experience in the teams, there are no overt comparative references to competence within the team membership. This assumption of collegial competence has to be understood in the following context of private and self- regulated practice.

'....I never tell the nasties....' Social control in the team

The teams operate on the basis of a 'company of equals' (see Freidson and Rhea, 1977), whereby colleagues' role performances are never entirely visible to the wider group which operates on assumptions of competence and courtesy. Should misdemeanours come to light these are dealt with discreetly in order to preserve the mutually advantageous notion of a membership that is equally capable. The child care workers believe in their own authority to determine case practices and even if colleagues have doubts about the propriety of another's conduct they refrain from making this apparent:

> ....we get on with our own cases, you wouldn't be very popular if you kept making suggestions even if you thought someone was going wrong....

All the team members are aware of the different biographical and occupational backgrounds among their colleagues. They have some idea of the varying abilities among team mates, yet the lack of divisive relations is a remarkably stable feature of team relationships. Team harmony is maintained through a subtly managed and daily negotiated order. For example, there are instances when workers receive complaints from clients about previous workers who have handled the same case. These complaints are rarely communicated to the worker concerned or other members of the team or office:

> child care worker: I've had nice and nasty comments (about team mates), but I'd never tell the

'nasties'. I mean I always defend a worker if a client says something. You know - I'd say, er, 'he's really not like that, he's very popular with clients'. I mean it's only the client's perception. We all work in such different ways. I picked up one of Chris's cases (Chris had left the office a month before) now I really work differently with that family, nothing like the way she did. She came down really hard on them, you know the Heaths?

researcher: Oh yes, they're the Irish family.

Um. You see Chris was a young girl. I'm forty. I'm a Celt like the Heaths and their attitudes to family life don't worry me as much as they did Chris. She was very directive with them....in fact if I'd had the case at the beginning I don't think there would have been the care order on the one and the supervision on the other (child). You see that was part of Chris's strong personality. She's very, er, perhaps too firm.

researcher: Er, say if Chris was here would you tell her how you feel about this case?

child care worker: No. If she'd been here I don't think I would have discussed it with her much. (wry laugh)

As the interview extract suggests, the worker prefers not to endanger the collegial assumptions of competence as this would undermine team harmony. This is not simply a feature of the team in question, all groups require some 'esprit de corps' of membership in order to cohere. This can be threatened by discrediting information about individuals or elements within the group (Moore and Tumin, 1949). That such information is rarely shared in the social work teams is also due to the typically unobserved

78

nature of day to day practice. On the occasions where colleagues do know about a practice they judge to be dubious they maintain a discreet silence and expect the same in return. As Goffman (1971, p.21) observes, participants in a communicative process are expected to restrain their 'heartfelt opinion' in order that the project at hand may proceed. The teams construct this veneer of consensus, an 'interactional modus vivendi' (Goffman *op cit.*) whereby members remain silent or neutral about matters not immediately important to themselves.

This notion of stable team harmony is not difficult to conceive given the members' shared claim to autonomy, competence and privileged knowledge of their own cases. For example, when a worker discusses her cases, team mates accept that the individual member is best placed to describe the circumstances of the moment. She has the 'authority to know'. This, as Mukerji (1976, p.65) observes, is given to the one who can 'display the most appropriate social characteristics relevant to the issue at hand'. This applies acutely in the context of social work teams. The worker's interventions are unobserved, the content of her caseload is largely unknown or partially shared with colleagues and consequently members are rarely in a position to challenge a team mate's view of individual case events.

Limited visibility of collegial performance can of course give rise to an alternative conception of the teams as a 'company of unequals' (Lorber and Satow, 1977) rather than equals. Given that workers govern their own pace and style of intervention it is possible that very different and unequal distributions of output may obtain. Nevertheless, even if such disparities are glimpsed, they are not voiced openly but kept within the quiet gossip of close colleagues:

team mate to colleague:	(sotto voce) I've been rushing round like mad this week and some of our lot (nods towards desk of absent colleague rather than naming her) never seem pushed.
colleague:	Yes I know what you mean but then *I've had* (her emphasis) an easy fortnight but things are starting blow a bit....

Workers may sometimes feel aggrieved if they gain the impression that others are not as busy as themselves. However, they can never know for certain and so their suspicions remain discreetly shared or not voiced at all. Furthermore, all workers know that work is the experience of changing tempo. There are lulls of quiet routine punctuated by unpredictable demands that quickly surface and precipitate an urgent response. As the second worker above notes, 'things are starting to blow a bit'. The variable pitch of demand creates strains and it is particularly during moments of feverish activity that workers display further clues to their identity as competent self-regulating practitioners. Crises and emergencies are testing experiences that mark a change in status for the practitioner. These crucial moments are milestones in occupational careers and have to be understood in the following context of a taxing and hostile occupational world.

Rites de passage: baptism through stress

It is essential to view the child care workers as embedded in processes of team membership whereby individual practitioners gradually acquire or glean clues about their colleagues and how they work. Over time, members learn about their team mates' abilities, interests and personal backgrounds. They do not do this through the formal semantics of social work knowledge. They do not 'talk' social work theory or methods. Instead, like many occupational groups (Strauss, 1977, pp.158-9), they use a 'lingo' or 'slang' to communicate shared experiences of the job. A core experience, and one well recognised within the occupation is a sense of pressure, uncertainty and sometimes fear. In the area office the workers deal with the stresses of the job by sharing their anxiety with others through the use of a specific occupational rhetoric.

Members can quickly summon attention from team mates in the form of an encouraging nod or sympathetic exchange. This is achieved through short-hand phrases that collapse the complexities of a difficult case into a recognisable and shared experience of occupational anxiety. By using this short-hand 'lingo' the worker achieves two things. First, she elicits an expression of support, secondly, such rhetoric affirms her membership of this 'special' collegial group, which, in the view of its members, bears the brunt of demands made upon the organisation. The use of the 'lingo' is a claim to this identity. It is they and not those 'higher up' who experience stress and it is the capable worker who manages anxiety without being disabled by fatigue or upset.

Observation in the office noted the use of phrases such as 'burnt out worker', cases 'blowing up' or 'blown'. Such terms instantly conjure up familiar experiences in the minds of team mates. The term 'blow' is used frequently to suggest that a case or cases are moving towards some state of crisis requiring urgent attention. A crisis is a critical moment for the worker, she has to act quickly (e.g., remove a child into care, investigate a suspicious injury to an infant, respond to a housing eviction or disconnection of domestic fuel where children are involved). In brief, the worker faces an unanticipated departure from intended routines. While the reasons for crises are diverse they are easily grasped by colleagues through a shared imagery of cases 'blowing', 'bubbling', 'simmering' and 'breaking down'. This notion of eruption and unpredictability, a seemingly volcanic metaphor for family problems, is a common theme of everyday brief exchanges between workers and can be noted in the common parlance of other social work agencies (see Blech, 1981, p.23).

Reference to these images of explosive family upsets allows a worker to convey quickly the present circumstances of her case or cases. In doing so she elicits a sympathetic response from nearby team mates:

> (A worker returns from a family visit, sits at her desk and sighs, she then directs her comments to the team in general)

> Oh God! Everything seems to be blowing at once (sighs).

> (Two colleagues pause and murmur appreciatively and return to their interrupted activities, a third colleague takes up the implicit request for attention: having secured a listener the worker continues)

> Three of my cases - you know the Jones one - are starting to break down and I'm going on leave tomorrow (continues to provide brief summation of case circumstances)

colleague:	Mine are pretty stable at the moment why don't you leave me their names and if anything comes up we can try and keep an eye on them, keep it going till you get back?
child care worker:	It's OK. I'll have a word with Joan (team leader) and if they do blow she'll know what I think and can get something done, they may be OK but you can never tell....

As the above colleague states, her cases are 'stable' and she can spare time to watch out for her team mate's cases. However, in this instance, as in most observed, the workers wish to share their worries rather than seek any personal intervention into their cases by a team mate. In the event that there is a crisis in an absent team mate's caseload the team leader would typically assess the issue, and if there were no alternative, instruct another team member to temporarily manage the matter. Talk of 'blow ups', of being 'under pressure', immediately communicate to others the speaker's engagement with arduous work and is one of the few means for sharing instant information about present work exigencies. Brief oral accounts versed in the rhetoric of anxiety and apprehension, serve to demonstrate that the worker 'knows' what 'work' is all about. Indeed the experienced practitioner is one who has gone through the baptism of a case or cases that have truly engaged her energies and emotions. This was aptly put by one of the team leaders:

> ....there's always pressure in this work but you learn to handle it, er, you learn through experience, every worker gets their 'case' that takes them to the end of their tether. All the team have had that experience - take Michelle, she's having the most dreadful time with this NAI, er, gone to Crown Court - cross examined - the parents hate her because she's taken the boy in (removed the child into residential care). She's under real pressure from the parents but she's still working with them, giving everything, despite the parents' feelings. Everyone gets their 'case' and this is hers. But she's still in there with the family and that's caring in my opinion....

The extract points to a decisive shift in the 'moral career' (Goffman, 1968, p.119) of the practitioner. She has experienced that most stressful of occupational events: non accidental injury to a child (NAI), leading to a court investigation of all the circumstances and her performance. However, she has 'proved' herself in the eyes of the supervisor, in that she persists with the family despite their hostile attitudes towards her. This ability to weather the occupational hazards and continue without being disabled by 'pressure' marks out the competent worker. The baptismal case is an occupational rite de passage. Yet, it is not so much the 'baptism' of harrowing circumstances, it is, as the team leader observes, the ability to persevere with this case and others. Once 'baptised' the worker still has to maintain her 'faith', that is, she must still take on and manage similar occupational hazards without departing from expected service ideals. This feature of the occupational experience finds some parallel with religious conversion. Here, Berger and Luckmann (1967, p.177-8) observe that it is not the conversion experience that is ultimately crucial but the ability to keep taking the conversion seriously. The new identity has to be cultivated and reinforced and a religious community provides the 'indispensable plausibility structure for the new reality' (Berger and Luckmann *op cit.*). Likewise the team colleagues provide a 'community' of sorts. Like other occupational groups (Gold, 1952; Dingwall, 1977) they share stories and swap comments that show they too are seasoned veterans who have undergone stress and danger but have carried on. They too are competent members of the team.

The occupational literature reinforces this imagery of stress and hazard. There is an addiction to metaphors that explicitly invoke the rigours of practice, for example practitioners are seen as battling 'at the front' or 'at the coal face' (Baird, 1981b) or 'in the firing line' (Blech, 1981) of service delivery. Indeed, throughout the period of observation I was regaled with accounts of desperate moments, of hysterical children, angry fathers, disconsolate mothers and tragic siblings. It is of course not surprising that members of an occupation will wish to justify their endeavours and, in doing so, draw on and emphasise the more arduous aspects of the task. Roth's (1972) observations of a hospital emergency service revealed that workers selected their more difficult cases when describing their work to those outside the membership. He noted that a close analysis of patient contact indicated that the examples offered by staff were not representative of their total clientele. The situation in the area office is very similar. While there are serious 'crises' and exhausted workers this is not the fate of all practitioners at all times. Rather, the notion of pressure and dramatic rhetoric contribute to a collective self-image that demonstrates the esprit de corps of child care practice. Lodged in the collective imagination is a view that work is tough and demanding and it takes a special kind of person to manage this and still provide a worthy service. It follows that only a competent and experienced practitioner can live in this elevated realm of practice. Within the team as a whole it is always likely that one of the members has a case that is moving towards crisis. The rest of the team are aware of this impending emergency and this creates a shared atmosphere of tension. These moments of crisis eclipse the many cases that are quietly managed and known largely to the individual worker.

Occupational rhetoric, myth and folk-lore are means of communicating and assuaging the discomforts of the job. Support and concern are part of this adaptive mechanism and criticism is reserved for those outside the friendly camp of team relationships. Nevertheless, whilst the occupational experience is one of changing tempo, there are days and weeks of comparative calm when workers catch up with their administrative duties. There are meetings to attend, other agencies to contact and occasional training courses to complete. The use of time is never closely examined by supervisory or managerial members. The practitioners do not have to account for time spent on specific tasks. If they work late in the evenings they take time off as convenient. They are not role-partners and hence team mates do not depend on colleagues to process cases, except in the event of severe crises and the absence of the worker concerned.

The practitioners are predominantly married women and, as several emphasise, they have to fit their domestic tasks into the working day. For example, there is shopping to do and the occasional need to take their children to dental and medical appointments. One worker described her daily chore of housework as preventing her arriving on time in the mornings and her compensation for this through evening work. Another described her reluctance to engage in evening visits in order to be home in time for her young family. Neither the office manager nor the team leaders seek to monitor closely workers' daily activities; they consider that the discretionary use of time is a necessary feature of the job. The 'good' worker will not abuse this facility. Indeed, the discretionary management of the working day is a much prized aspect of the job for these working mothers and wives who meet domestic as well as occupational demands:

child care worker
to student: In this job we like to get about, we like
                               the freedom to come and go - get in the
                               car and zoom off! We may moan about
                               the job but we wouldn't swap it for a job
                               in admin, nine to five, no time for
                               shopping or getting the kids off (laughs)
                               but you make up for it in the evening
                               mind (evening visits to consumers).

Thus, while the workers can easily invoke the dramatic occupational rhetoric to describe work experience to those 'outside', they can on reflection comment on the 'freedom' to manage time flexibly in the settled periods between emergencies and hectic activity:

child care worker
to team mate: Things have been going great for weeks,
                               now everything's going haywire, late
                               nights all this week....

The management of time is rarely determined by forward planning, apart from a week or so. Like other workers (Satyamurti, 1981, p.141; p.152) they believe that unpredictable events prevent arrangements and appointments too far ahead and believe the 'client' is likely to forget an appointment some weeks hence. Practitioners, at my request, showed their work diaries and these confirmed that they had few plans to visit consumers beyond the next week or ten days. Instead short-term appointments or simply dropping in on consumers typifies the planning of visits. The child care workers believe that their tasks can not be neatly punctuated by set activities at set times and there are no official procedures for imposing such a routine.

Their occupational world is a mixture of two crucial temporal processes. They experience the job as 'here and now', that is, tackling the problems of the moment and responding to occasional emergencies. Their reluctance to plan further than the next few days or week collapses the occupational horizon into a closely drawn world of immediacy. Yet it is over the months and years that they imperceptibly acquire a sedimented common-sense knowledge about themselves, their colleagues and those they visit and this informs the immediate world of daily practice.

Within this complex temporal frame the practitioners learn that the collective self-image is one of the competent solo-practitioner. The worker engages with the consumers unobserved by team mates but draws on the membership for support. While they share in the dilemmas and anxieties of practice they manage their own cases devoid of intrusive scrutiny by colleagues. This delicate blend of unseen interventions and a shared colleague network of support is the carefully negotiated order of team membership. The competent worker quickly learns the expectations of colleagueship which centres around the harmonious reciprocities of mutual and uncritical concern. While the team member is never assessed in any formal or deliberately overt sense by her team mates, she nevertheless understands her role on the basis of shared but rarely articulated assumptions about the able practitioner. This is a worker who responds sympathetically and without intrusion to team mates' problems. She manages her own cases and carefully looks to her personal skills, energies and resources. The able worker copes with stress and continues providing a service. These facets of the good worker are understood by the competent team member.

Ten years later

At the time of writing this addendum the office was dealing with around 550 cases, some fifty cases less than a decade before. Such numbers resist simple comparison because of departmental changes in administrative categories; reductions in the use of residential care; a shift in practice towards short term child protection and markedly less involvement in what might loosely be described as open-ended preventative work that featured more prominently a decade or more ago. This said, the number of cases involving children in the care of the local authority had not changed significantly in relation to the national average at 1987 and 1997. However, the number of child protection registrations had, according to the department's own estimations, moved significantly above the national average during the period since local government reorganisation in 1996. Also, the number of referrals requiring a full investigation of actual or suspected abuse of a child had doubled in the last few years. The reasons for this dramatic rise in child protection work were beyond the scope of this enquiry but for the workers the cause lay partly in wider demographic and cultural changes surrounding family life that increased domestic instability. They also attributed some of the rise in protection work to the social and economic decline they saw in the communities they visited. Most however were of the view that the increase could in some measure be laid at the very door of protection practice itself and the response this called forth from staff and management. As one worker said: 'the work here is task centred child safety, then safety for me and safety for the agency, that's work today'. Such imperatives had their impact on the atmosphere of the setting and relations in the colleague group as sketched below:

> ....work does feel like a war zone sometimes - but here (office) feels a safe place, there's a lot of humour, more aggressive humour about those outside - and we are sometimes jokey or flippant with each other about the families we see - we sort of egg each other on, and we get too flippant and I don't want to get like this - even though we don't mean it, and know we don't mean it....

This comment from a worker in the long term team broadly expressed a view that would be shared by most in the office. Work was demanding and sometimes corrosive of the concern and empathy for clients that might ideally be expected of people doing this job. Problems with cases or other agencies were often too numerous or too perplexing to resolve other than through a certain bleak humour that only those engaged in this business can fully appreciate. In this respect the atmosphere of the office shared certain affinities with the world of their predecessors in that work as stress, danger or numbing frustration never strayed far from day to day conversation. If anything, the impression was that this was much more pronounced than before, no doubt because of the nature of the work and because the small open plan office facilitated the quick transmission of news about troublesome cases or worrying encounters. Also, the short term team responding largely to urgent referrals, was the daily source of shared or overheard conversations about some serious investigation or other. Similarly, the long term team in dealing with those cases that required ongoing intervention, were typically involved with families where crisis and breakdown frequently created a sense of drama and anxiety. Those few workers operating as full time duty workers at reception were even more exposed to the exigencies of family life that could without much warning appear before them and quickly engage their full attention. This point was cogently put by one of these duty workers who having read the original chapter on colleague relationships observed:

....I recognised the chapter easily, lots of things around colleague stuff, and how we don't know much about each others' cases. I also got the thing about pressure and stress as something that dominates us, but I think it's more than then. It's not the same now, we do much more emergency protection, here and now stuff, constantly busy. I think we have created the demand by the way we respond, we seem to treat everything as an emergency, we're in a constant state of anxiety. Today we check and re-check our decisions, there's not the same flexibility now, we're so accountable - it causes doubts, self doubts. And I think we're not so close with our colleagues, we don't seem to have time to develop a shared view of what we should be doing as an office, we just jump (pauses). We don't as a rule have time for therapeutic work, we may try to connect clients to that, but we don't do it, so we don't measure ourselves in relation to that sort of work, things have changed since your book, we measure against the safety of the child. It's a change I don't like. I know I don't handle change too well but I used to like working here, now we seem to be chasing our tails (pauses) people want out (pauses) often I feel I can't go and work one more day....

For this worker, as for most, the key issue was not whether some intervention or other was successful in relation to an aspect of family functioning but rather whether or not the procedures for ensuring the safety of a child thought likely to be exposed to some abuse were in place. More therapeutic endeavours were not on the agenda for most workers as will be illustrated in later chapters, rather, success for them was typically cast around managing risks associated with the child remaining in or near some source of possible or actual harm. In this context, the expectations of staff towards the office as a place of safety for themselves in an otherwise difficult if not hostile occupational environment, was an understandable feature of their assumptions about everyday work. Yet, the office world was experienced differently according to exposure to the daily demands around child protection investigations. Those at the 'front line' might have greater dependency upon the office as a place of support and would understandably be less sanguine about any shortcomings in this regard - a point put with some intensity by one duty worker:

> It doesn't feel very safe working here right now, there's no real management to speak of, those that are around are too pushed to be there when you need them. We get into our little support systems to cope - my networks are important to me, they cut across teams - it's about trust and who you can trust to get the right support. Morale is pretty low at present. When you get to management it's a fairly knee-jerk interpretation. Management reacts to every problem - often short sharp and heavy, no risks taken, no creative work. We all get sucked into the drama of some instant reaction....

This sense of being an 'emergency service' was echoed by those in the short term team who would follow up most of the referrals that came from the duty desk. Most described how they worked far beyond their contracted hours in order to respond to what they perceived as an unending queue of urgent referrals. They knew that they were not officially required to do this extra work, they also knew there was no departmental edict that somehow demanded that work be conducted in a highly charged atmosphere of emergency. This point was bluntly put by one member of the short term team:

> I get the feeling that if we had more staff we would still take on more and more work because we don't know how to work with risk. It's about risk and how we should take responsibility - it's

not a matter of policy, no one's said this is how we must work. It's not policy but the philosophy of the managers that tends to pervade the whole system. They're worried about making mistakes. We've had meetings with the Director and we said we can't go on like this. He said we're not expected to do the impossible or work over the hours but that was just talk. Nothing changes. I am not given permission *not* (speaker's emphasis) to do anything, you know, what I can leave undone. We all feel we have to examine everything or else we feel we are acting in dangerous ways....

A strong sense of disaffection seemed to exist for several of the duty and short term staff over the way work had become akin to, as one respondent put it, 'a family fire brigade service'. Much of the blame for this was laid upon particular managers who were seen as either driven by the excitement of crisis and/or by the fear of failure. Yet at the same time there was genuine affection by most respondents for their office managers who were seen as industrious and committed as anyone else. Several of those in the long term team also described a world where crisis and emergency made for gruelling hours of work well beyond the terms of employment:

I think there is a sort of moral pressure put on us by some managers to work over the odds, but no one ever says to them 'sorry I'm going home', and the managers work as hard as the rest of us, probably more. We've actually had a meeting with the Director and he said he didn't expect anyone to work over their hours. Shows you how little he knows about work here. You can't just dump on your colleagues. If you say 'no' the next person is going to be asked. If I was going to take off all my time in lieu I would be doing a four day week for months! You're under pressure to offer goodwill as an employee, it's the culture here. It's not 5pm and you're finished, you feel guilty if you go, and those in the short term team are always there late. So, if a case comes up at gone 5pm you work with it, you are not asked to, you just take it, it's a kind of moral pressure....

Similar accounts were offered by other staff. For example, one assistant social worker described how when she first joined the office she quickly learned that people work some if not most of their lunch hour, 'when I first came I used to go home for my lunch hour and then I began to detect that this was not what you did - it was sort of frowned upon, not in some overt

89

way, but you got the feeling that it was not the done thing'. The team managers were well aware that staff gave more of their time and energy than was officially required, but not because they, the managers, asked for this, but because the demands made upon the office called forth goodwill from everyone in order to manage the pressing matters that surfaced most days:

> My team runs on goodwill, it shouldn't but it does. We all work hard. I'm like the team leader in your book, I take referrals home every night to plan for the next day. I take work home on week-ends. I'm almost on duty twenty four hours a day and I'm not sure I can go on like this. I'm making important decisions, really important decisions on the hoof, sometimes running between meetings and (child protection) conferences. Everyone works over the hours. People aren't happy I know, but they have to know there's no easy solution, there's not going to be any more resources....

Such views from staff and managers were not some artful fiction or exaggeration for the benefit of outsiders. Observation over several weeks revealed many instances of unsocial hours being worked that were never compensated by time off. All staff seemed exposed to the office culture of extended hours, all were touched in some way by the drama and urgency of events around them. All knew work to be a mixture of hectic intervention with families and more reflective work on case recording and planning but rarely with a comfortable balance between these activities. Apart from the daily arrival of new referrals there were still unallocated cases to be dealt with arising from unfilled vacancies in the teams; here then was a reserve army of clients ready to absorb any spare capacity:

> What your chapter didn't have is the sort of vacancies we have today. There's a lot of unallocated cases because we've lost staff through early retirement and we've been holding a vacancy for ages. My cases are quiet at the moment so I will be getting some of (names retired worker) cases now. And the short-term team has never been full ever! That's almost two years!

Against this backdrop of an unending and insistent demand, brought sharply into focus by the worrying events in one's own case or that of a nearby worker, there lay only the colleague group as a bulwark against the

90

troubles of the day. Here though were some notable differences from the world of ten years ago where the team itself was a well bounded entity in which all could expect some degree of support. First, it is essential to appreciate the compressed and tense nature of the office environment, with a membership who saw little in the way of effective management beyond their own locale, and where the new department was itself only a small fraction of the former organisation with consequent reduction in resources. The sense of being a thin and isolated line of workers holding out against a tide of unstable families reflects reasonably the way staff saw their world. This sense of working as one practitioner said, 'in a pressure cooker', would expose any fault lines that existed within the colleague group. This it did, more so than was ever observed in the setting of ten years ago. Now, workers seemed much more selective about friendships and more likely to seek those they felt happier with, particularly in a setting where views might collide about the very nature of practice itself and about the qualities of the practitioner. This occurred despite most workers knowing little of the cases held by colleagues or ever having observed staff with clients. Nonetheless, they had some idea of the broad orientation of another's practice and how this fitted their own way of doing things:

I wouldn't really know whose cases were whose, or if they did any more work with them than me. I don't visit with anyone much but I pick up a little when someone's on the phone. We're all under pressure, everyone works hard and you tend to discuss with people you *expect* (speaker's emphasis) support from - that's not necessarily your team mates. Basically, we're split here between those that want to intervene in families and those who don't, and that cuts across teams. Some of us want to patch the family up and some want to deal with the child only and so there are different approaches here. We are all child centred but some are more focused around the child than others. I feel quite happy about most people here but we're more in cliques and networks than teams....

The pattern of relations in the setting did seem to reflect this view. That is, staff were not required to form themselves into distinct team clusters but were scattered in groups of three and four throughout the open plan office. During their daily routines workers would often pause to share matters with other small groups or individuals as much as with their immediate neighbours. This much was self evident and observed by the team managers, one of whom stated 'there's no rivalry between the teams, but there are lots of cross cutting friendships, which is a good thing...'. While there were no rivalries between teams there were some underlying tensions as one short term team member observed:

> We've had a movable population of workers in recent years - it (office) is not a homogenous group here - it's not necessarily a warm environment. There are conflicting dynamics - but warm within small groups and networks. People don't criticise one another openly, that's done in the network. Some of it can be quite a heavy undercurrent, it can be corrosive. But we sort out our own problems here, the team managers wouldn't always know what's going on (pauses)....they're so busy....

Another worker in the long-term team made similar observations:

> There are some difficult people here - just normal human nature I guess - but there are groups within teams, often around the way you work, some are very direct with clients and assertive, deal only with the child, is it safe? Me, I'm more inclined to the broader family, still concerned for the child, and I think there are differences there a bit. But I'd say we are a pretty solid group across the office.

A more heartfelt note was offered by one of the full time duty workers who considered that the root of any antagonism between colleagues lay in the nature of the work itself and that the constant barrage of protection enquiries had created strains on relations in the short term team. This had resulted in a suggestion by someone for a team building session in order to remedy whatever discontent might exist:

> We're a bit caught up in a whinging process because of the work, so there's going to be a team building day on how to handle pressure of work - someone said we'd do better to find out how we can like each other before going on to team building to deal with pressure - I thought that sums it up. We used to share more before, now it's selective sharing as opposed to a sharing culture.

These sorts of comments describe office relations some distance from those observed a decade ago. While there were many similarities, there was the vital difference of the invasive influence of child protection work on collegial relationships and identities. This was an influence that seemed to generate differing if not conflicting views between staff on how to respond to risk in a climate of uncertainty and possible blame. Such a climate seemed to undermine the easy trust and openness that was plainly visible within the two teams of ten years ago. Some of the reasons for this will be illustrated more clearly in the following chapters. At this point however it is important not to create some picture of the overall staff group as riven by various unspoken and deep antagonisms. This would be a serious distortion, for the setting was broadly a supportive and well mannered environment. As one recent recruit, a non qualified member of staff noted, 'I was surprised when I joined the team about how much respect I was given, how I was welcomed, my opinion seemed to matter, even at the bottom of the ladder'.

The insights of those on the lower organisational rungs can be valuable, they often see or hear things in the company of those somewhat higher which the latter would not often display to someone of equal or senior rank. For example, unqualified staff would often go with qualified team mates to visit a family if the seriousness of events warranted the security of two workers. Here, they would see what few other workers would normally witness, a colleague 'at work with clients':

> When I read your chapter I thought yes! This is where I work! I saw a lot in it, but then I thought a bit more. There's changes. Like I go out with the team on visits, I occasionally see the different techniques they have - some you think well that's pretty forceful - knocking the door and coming on strong - others quite gentle - and I often work with them (families) later on my own. And they say, don't you ever let so and so (team mate) back in my house! Like you said, 'I never tell the nasties', well I do but in a nice way. Sort of make a joke of it. But then I'm unqualified - how can I challenge?

As with colleagues a decade earlier, criticism over another's handling of a case, as this unqualified worker observed, was typically not a matter to be shared directly. This applied to qualified and unqualified alike. If views were expressed they were more likely to be in the form of some humorous exchange as noted by one qualified worker in the short term team: 'we quip about people's capacities - as a form of banter - we wouldn't just talk behind their backs, but we wouldn't confront a colleague, that's a matter for management'. Yet there was one area of work, not evident ten years ago, over which many respondents stated their willingness to challenge a colleague, this was in respect of anti-discriminatory practice. The influence of this area of professional activity which has come much more to prominence in the 1990s, was according to respondents, keenly felt within the colleague group. Most declared their readiness to challenge any gesture made by peers that might offend this tenet of practice. Here then was a significant area over which more overt displays of criticism might be aired:

> I don't think the workers in your book would have been trained in anti discriminatory practice (ADP) like most of us. We've come up over the last five years and it was a big part of the course (Diploma in Social Work). I'd challenge some colleagues over ADP - others, such as unqualified, well I'd feel a bit elitist challenging them - you have to explain. But you can do it in different ways, jokey, straight, ironic. If we have discrimination here it's never blatant, more subtle if at all. I think we're self-regulating over ADP. We would all show in no uncertain terms that it was inappropriate and jump on it quickly. It's only happened a few times with (pauses) well with one or two who know better now....

While the workers could not easily regulate the demands made upon them or depart from the case management mode of dealing with child abuse and its risks, they could, as the above extract suggests, impose some control over the moral environment they occupied by dealing judiciously and quickly with any discriminatory practice they deemed unacceptable. If this was any consolation in an otherwise volatile world it was not immediately apparent. For the most part, they seemed too hard pressed to worry overly about any unwise utterances by colleagues and were typically consumed by events in their own cases. Like a decade ago, they knew little of one another's cases, they knew however which of their colleagues practised in ways similar to themselves and most chose to seek advice or support accordingly. The choice of friend or informal consultant appeared more deliberate than before. The sense of pressure, of cases blowing, the dramatic imagery of family crisis was there as before but much more insistent. The office world seemed more tense, less open and affectionate, and more closely delineated around small self-selected groups than ever witnessed a decade before.

5 Supervisory relations and the discreet art of assessment

Social work is indelibly marked by role insulation and undefined areas of organisational activity. Workers manage their own cases and see little of their colleagues' practices with consumers. Likewise those placed higher in the organisation have even less access to the routines of lower participants. However, the team leader is intentionally instituted to assess and guide practice. Yet, as will be demonstrated, her role is also characterised by insulation and unobserved strategies that secure particular objectives around team harmony and practice evaluation. For example, she can withhold information from local and higher managers about unsatisfactory worker performance in order to resolve this matter within the discreet dyad of worker and supervisor. In doing so, any unwanted intrusion from above is avoided and the team also remains unaware of any individual's shortcomings, which in turn helps sustain the notion of a company of equals. Furthermore, she can hold her own private view of practitioner abilities and this will influence the way she allocates new cases and manages the team. For example, those deemed less capable may not receive certain cases, yet they and their colleagues may remain unaware of this. Such manoeuvres are deemed necessary for the following reasons.

At the nub of the supervisory process is the delicate matter of social control. Charged with the task of providing guidance and advice, supervisors also have to ensure that specific standards are maintained. In the course of this they have to rely upon the workers to provide some account of their unobserved interventions. The team leaders do not witness the workers' practices with their clients. Such insulation is not peculiar to social work and in all organisations some degree of unobserved activity is essential to accomplish tasks without undue and unpredictable interference (Merton, 1968, p.398). Yet as Coser (1964) notes, too much unobserved activity exempted from evaluation can lead to variable and unacceptable standards. Consequently, in the child care teams it is the fine balance of polite enquiry into the work of practitioners, who see themselves as self-regulating, that marks out the able team leader.

It will be shown that the two supervisors in the child care team are adept at managing the above requirements. Like the 'good' supervisors observed in other organisations (Blau and Scott, 1963, p.155), they demonstrate to their teams their independence from higher management and their disinclination to intrude overly on the workers' day to day practices. They engage in a delicate blend of reciprocal dependencies. For example, the workers depend on supervisors for advice and support, protection from higher scrutiny and the private resolution of performance problems that do not injure member conceptions of competence. This much is recognised by the office manager and his deputy who have themselves been practitioners and supervisors in the earlier part of their welfare careers. They appreciate the complexities of the supervisory role and are content to leave matters of practitioner conduct to the team leaders:

area office manager: The team leaders are protectors and evaluators. I suspect the team leaders have probably a better evaluation of their staff than perhaps they will tell me. They will give me an honest and reasoned evaluation of their best staff but I think they censor some of their comments about the worst staff and protect the worst staff from me while they try and bring on their skills - so they're a bit in the middle, it's a difficult role and I've been through it myself....really I leave it up to them to tell me about any problems they've got in the team....

It will be shown that the supervisors, like others in people-processing organisations (Blau, 1964, p.38), allow the workers to violate certain expectations and thereby gain the trust and obligation of team members. This supervisory discretion does not simply occur because of close relations between leader and team but because of dependencies that derive from unobserved practice. The team leaders are forever reliant upon the members to provide an account of their interventions and this, they consider, will be forthcoming if the workers can anticipate a helpful and unabrasive response. The supervisory relationship does not entail the instrumental use of affect as a means of obtaining deeper insights into unobserved practice.

The genuine sympathy for the workers stems from the supervisors' own experience of doing the job. This shared baseline of occupational background lends credibility to the team leaders' claims that they are not 'management' and are not like 'pen-pushers' in other parts of the city department. The team leaders see themselves as the guardians of good practice. They are there to defend their service ideals against the encroachment of incompatible objectives emanating in their view from higher management. Their fear is that they might get out of touch with the experience of managing clients and cases. Rarely visiting consumers themselves they are always open to the opprobrium heaped on those who never face the clientele or the 'pressure' of the job. Hence it is understandable that the team leaders endorse the team assumption that practitioners are the cornerstone of the organisational service and too often unappreciated:

I always make sure I'm available during the day for the team. They can come in with any query and I'm here. In the evening I catch up with the admin - it's the only way I can work....you see the real work's out there in the field - that's where the real issues are. The social workers are out there and the pressure's on them - not me - but I'm here all of the time for them.

Strong loyalty to the team is evinced by both supervisors. They express the necessity of a team ethos of care and support in order to manage the demands of the job. They sustain the morale of the membership and provide a model for their view of service ideals:

....if we can't look after one another then what can we do for the client? They have to know they can come and talk to me about anything. I'm here to hear their problems at work and at home - it all affects what they do.

The supervisors view social work as a life encompassing project that is very much determined by biographical and domestic facets of the individual worker. Intimate knowledge of the practitioners' private lives is not excluded from considerations about their occupational performance and is a topic that may be easily raised in the course of supervisory encounters. The team leaders assiduously maintain a sentiment of diffuse concern for the social workers. They are available throughout the day and can be observed hovering by the team, talking, encouraging, eager to listen to any difficulties and offering brief enquiries into the troublesome or topical issues of the private and occupational lives of the membership.

The supervisors subscribe to the shared view that all the team are competent workers. While they know there are different abilities and skills within the team they skilfully avoid an explicit statement to this effect. Indeed it was not until some months had passed that they provided confidential opinions about the practitioners that were never shared outside the research interview. The supervisors recognise that a divisive or competitive membership will offend the core conceptions of able practitioner and they play down differences in competence. Overt and invidious distinctions within the team will make for defensive relationships and a reluctance to reveal those unobserved practices that might be judged as confirmation of a worker's inferior status in the team. Indeed the supervisors also recognise that there are members of the team with experience and skills that match, if not exceed, their own. Thus supervisors could also be judged as less competent in a membership that endorsed open and outspoken evaluation of abilities. Consequently the team leaders prefer to manage the supervisory relationships within the unobserved confines of individual encounters. They resolve the disparities within the membership by invoking their own role as 'first among equals', and the 'equals' are viewed as 'equal but different'. This cements team relationships and secures the collegial self-image of capable, self-regulating practitioner:

team leader:	....all the team have different strengths and weaknesses, they're at different stages of development so you can't really say one is better than the other, do you see? I think social workers get criticised enough. It's very easy to do that, er, we have closer relationships here. My husband comes here sometimes, he says it's like a cloying womb! (laughs) but we care about one another and we rely on one another....

'Caring' is a core conception of service ideals within the occupation and it is a routine feature of the job that the supervisor will, through the medium of therapeutic care, attempt to remedy the shortcomings of a practitioner (Blech, 1981, p.7). It is also evident that a profession will typically resolve internally any problems of a poor service and seek to minimise public loss of confidence (Goode, 1957). Yet while this occurs through supervision, it may also occur beyond the scrutiny of higher authorities in the welfare organisation. Thus, while the corrective role of the supervisor is a recognised feature of the occupation, it is not well recognised that the nature of supervisory dependencies may deflect attention from deficiencies in social work practice. Protecting staff from the critical scrutiny of higher management is an implicit component of the supervisory role and proves fidelity towards the team. The team leaders' need for a trusting rapport with team members in order to share in their unobserved practice precludes an open and critical appraisal of work. It submerges inappropriate practice within the occupational shibboleth of supervisory care and support.

The following extracts from an interview with one of the team leaders illustrates this protective function. It also demonstrates that the team leader will discreetly resolve an issue without recourse to other members in the office. The extract refers to a practitioner who has written a letter to a mother who has been requesting her child's removal into residential care. The worker does not wish to accede to this demand. In order to make the parent fully appreciate the implications of her request, the worker is attaching to the letter some official forms for the mother to read, enter details and sign. The point at issue is that the forms are internal documents to be completed only by practitioners. This attempt to 'shock' the mother into changing her mind by making her fill in the official form and thereby contemplate the seriousness of her request, is ruled inappropriate by the team leader:

team leader: ....this job's about caring and we have to trust one another. I don't go running to them (managers) every time there's a problem. You see they (team members) have to know they can come and see me and talk openly. That's the only way you can do the work. Look (points to letter) read this. This is something you have to watch for (pauses while letter is read). Yes? Now you see the *social worker* (her emphasis) has to complete the forms not the client! What she's doing is insisting the client takes responsibility and realises what she's asking for, right? She's trying to make the mother sign the forms and fill them, so she realises what she's doing, that she's actually sending her

	child away! But you can't do that, you can't do that, you can't send forms out and use forms in this way. You see the child shouldn't come into care but we shouldn't let clients fill in forms - we should do that - do you see? She's trying to make the mother appreciate what she's doing, but that's the wrong way. Now if this letter was seen by (the office manager) he would certainly reject it, she'll have to try a different tack.
researcher:	What will you say to Liz? (worker)
team leader:	Well I respect her, the way she works. She does her best but you see I've known her for years. We're friends really. But she could get into trouble if the press saw this, but I'll be firm with her, this can't go out....

Not unlike the physician supervisor identified by Goss (1961) and Freidson (1975, p.210), the team leader reconciles the strains of supervising those who see themselves as self-regulating by asserting her loyalty to the normative ideals of the membership. Thus, she will not upset the prevailing assumptions that all are competent practitioners, she will have a 'talk' with the worker and quietly resolve the matter. The team leaders are aware that some workers are more able than other team colleagues, yet they protect practitioners from sharp criticism and collective knowledge of their shortcomings. By deft inter-personal tactics they preserve the worker's sense of status, as, for example, when supervisors describe how they allocate new cases in light of their private views of practitioner ability. Thus cases that are deemed highly sensitive and likely to elicit the gaze of significant others (departmental hierarchy, court appearance) due to serious circumstances, are directed to some rather than other workers:

team leader:	I have to get to know their strengths, like I said they're all pretty good, there's two, er, I won't mention names, who I don't think could handle a nasty NAI and if one comes up I sort of steer it to someone else.
researcher:	Can you give me an example?

team leader:	Well, (pauses) well all right, take Debra, she's excellent with her own cases but I don't think she's got the composure or that firmness you need when a child's in danger and you've got to whip it out. She's always busy, dedicated, and if something urgent comes up like investigating a battering (NAI) then I'll approach someone else, call them into the office (team leader's office).
researcher:	What about team meetings when you give out the new cases?
team leader:	Well I don't actually 'do' anything. I sort of see who is willing to take the cases and if it's not suitable for one or two of them I look to the others. I can't describe it really I sort of get them to ask for the case, or drop a few hints (laughs) it's hard to say....

This delicate allocation of cases is a means of protecting the 'Debras' from moving beyond their sphere of ability and this in turn protects the team from any scrutiny stemming from a poorly managed intervention by a less able worker. The subtle manoeuvre of matching cases to workers is accomplished without direct reference to the skills or abilities of the assembled workers at team meetings. Instead allocation proceeds through gestures, hints and the emergent responses of the moment. This finds some similarity with Satyamurti's (1981, p.51) description of the allocation process, where she suggests that cases are distributed on the basis of the supervisor's knowledge of the workers and their ability to withstand the stress of the particular case. The processes of reception, documentation and allocation of new cases are not investigated here but have been fully analysed from a phenomenological viewpoint by Smith (1980). The concern here is the interactive skills of the team leader, and a subtle allocation of cases is just one of the many arts of supervising social workers.

The team leaders are most pertinently grasped as ever engaged in a balancing act between their own and the team's dependencies. The practitioners depend upon them to endorse the shared notion that 'real' work is entrepreneurial and self-regulating practice 'out there' with consumers. The team leaders endorse the practitioner viewpoint of 'caring' as a dominant expression of good practice, and demonstrate this in their supervisory relationships. Additionally, the team leaders crucially depend upon the workers for an open account of their unobserved endeavours in order to determine the progress of cases and practitioner. Towards this end, it is essential to construct a private arena; a misericord where omissions and indiscretions can be revealed without fear of abrasive criticism. In a sense the supervisory encounter and relationship does not 'allow' the worker to be incompetent. Instead indiscretions and anxieties are massaged and managed in the warm ambience of supervisory support.

The pervasive ethic of 'care', of gently 'working through' problems of performance is a functional adjunct to solving the structural invisibility of intervention. More revealing accounts of unobserved performance might not be forthcoming in an assertive authority relationship. Consequently the practitioner does not face disagreeable sanctions when she admits to discreditable activities. Instead she 'confesses' and in return receives the absolution of considerate understanding. The following extract amply illustrates the 'confessional' aspect of supervisory relations and the affirmation of the core service ideal of 'care', both within the supervision process and in respect of consumer relations. It concerns a worker who has admitted to losing her temper with a consumer. Her confession does not elicit censure, instead her admission proves her recognition of poor practice and the team leader helps absolve her indiscretion. Indeed, they make sense of the event by invoking the ready caveat of 'pressure'. They then reconstruct the misdemeanour as ultimately 'evidence' of the worker's underlying good intentions. The display of ill-tempered behaviour is recast as palpable fact that the worker does care about the family as only one who 'cares' would feel strongly enough to show their emotional concern in this way. Indeed other practitioners (Mattinson and Sinclair, 1980, p.211) have sought to justify displays of anger towards clients in the belief that this is 'therapeutic'. It indicates that the worker, too, is human and not some 'superhuman' emissary. The team leader makes a similar point.

> ....you see a couple of weeks ago Jill was thinking of leaving, constant pressure. Er, two days ago she returned from a visit - difficult family - she's spent months getting them back on their feet - very disorganised lot - and when she went back the other day they had slipped back into the same old mess, kids screaming, they hadn't learned anything - no movement at all. Just back in the same old mess and Jill lost her temper got up and walked out! (laughs) She was overwrought but you see she had displayed temper to the client, she'd displayed emotion, she

was showing she cared for them. Anyway she came back to the office and told me all about it. Well we had to laugh - she'd worked so hard with them, but I know she cares she'll go back there and sort it out....

This account was confirmed by the worker in question some weeks later during an interview with the researcher in which she included the following comment, unprompted, in a long discussion about her relationships with consumers:

....for example, I'd left a family saying 'do what you bloody well like!' (laughs). Now that wasn't good social work but I was able to tell Jean (supervisor) about it - you see that's not me swearing at clients and walking out - I don't work like that but I'd had enough! I told Jean (supervisor) about it but it didn't go on the record, that would look a bit bad (laughs) but I did tell her. She knows me - the way I work - I can tell her anything....

Shortcomings, failures and anxieties can all be remedied in the supervisory process. In the above instance the written record will not contain the event and the managers and the team will remain unaware of the misdemeanour. This, typically, is the way performance problems are managed in the setting. Crucial to this process is what the supervisor 'knows' about the worker and the way she works. In this instance the participants draw upon their respective knowledge of the other in order to cast the event as a departure from the worker's usual style of practice. The worker's good record, lodged in the memory of the supervisor, outweighs the indiscretion. This reliance on the worker herself, rather than the circumstances of the misdemeanour, forms the basis on which the issue is judged. As the worker says, 'She knows me - the way I work', thus her known capacity as a 'good' worker offsets the event. Similar processes can be observed in other occupations. For example, Manning (1979b, p.174) speaks of 'trust credits' built up by long-serving policemen who are 'known' as usually reliable, and this is set against the occasional violation of rules and expectations. The social worker above has accumulated such 'credits'; some of the other workers have not and the manner of their assessment will now be considered.

Processes of supervisory control

The experience of daily work has been depicted so far as the outcome of a negotiable order in relation to organisational and collegial properties of the setting. There are of course non-negotiable elements surrounding questions of practice and a crucial feature here is the appropriate focus of attention in respect of intervention. Social workers agree and supervisors insist that practice focuses upon the 'family' or 'individuals' therein. While practitioners acknowledge that their interventions are informed by a casework tradition, they state they have insufficient time to engage in deeply intimate encounters. Instead all refer to a mixture of on the job experience and casework elements to construct a 'caring relationship', enabling them to explore domestic circumstances and search for 'problems' and 'solutions'. This will be discussed fully in Chapter Six. The question at this point is not whether these activities are actually 'caring' or 'therapeutic' but how they are seen as appropriate or otherwise. To this end the following comments of a team leader suggest that unobserved practice is made visible within the context of specific identities:

> ....you see the team work in their own ways, Joan would work with the whole family, er, that's the way she sees it, some would work one to one with clients, some do what I call supportive work, er, get resources as much as they can as well as making a relationship. I can't say which is best - it's a different approach they all have. I don't see Joan's working like that means she is working more deeply - I don't see it like that, er, another person might go along and just hold a hand and talk and that's valid, er, it can do as much work. It's a different way of working they all have and I appreciate the *way* (her emphasis) they're doing it....

That social work involves practitioner preference for certain styles of intervention is well known to the occupation (Sackville *et al.,* 1978, pp.6-7). What is more significant in the extract is the supervisor's reference to the 'way' work is performed rather than the method of work itself. During the interviews both the child care supervisors described their view of appropriate work by reference to service ideals of care and commitment. In essence the unobserved encounter is made visible and satisfactory when workers display their conformity to these service shibboleths. This however rarely occurs in some doctrinal statement by the worker but exists implicitly in the way she describes her encounters with consumers.

Unobserved work is assessed in relation to certain attributes within the worker herself. The evaluation of practice is inseparable from an evaluation of the practitioner and the supervisor looks for displays of conformity to the diffuse service ethic of care. These are typically gestural and tacit indications made by the practitioner that she is the 'right sort of person'. This is not just a feature of social work. In organisations generally there is as Ditton (1977, p.27) notes, a search by the experienced hand for the neophyte's innate competence and 'natural' suitability. In the area office, this is gathered in the practitioner's oral accounts of unobserved work and also in the countless observations and ad hoc exchanges between worker and supervisor over time:

> ....some of the team are fairly new and it takes time to get to know them and their cases, now Melanie's been here a few months. She's new to fieldwork and you might think she's a bit, er, abrupt when she talks about clients, but she's very good really, once you get to know how she works. She's had some hard cases and she's stayed in there working closely with the clients. You see, it's not what the job's doing to me or what the clients are doing to me but what I can *give* (her emphasis). If you can get that twist that's good social work - in there with the families....

The team leader has to get 'to know' the worker over time hence assessment does not stem from the instant matching of activity to a set of programmes or procedures. There are of course matters of official rules that may be discussed, negotiated or enforced in the management of cases and the team leader may play a part in this. However, the aspect of satisfactory practice surrounding unobserved work is typically gleaned in the gradual process of the supervisor learning about the motives and attitudes of the worker. This finds similarity with Dingwall's (1976) observation of health visitor training. Here, Dingwall notes that assessment does not simply address how tasks are carried out but the way tasks are accomplished in a manner that is deemed a proper performance by the right type of person. As Dingwall says (1976, p.338) it is the 'running together of doing and being', of accomplishing competent practice and competent practitioner.

The primacy of a caring and committed relationship is endorsed by the team leaders as the cornerstone of practice and can be seen in the responses of those who teach and supervise trainee practitioners (Syson, 1981, p.144). The supervisors are not so much concerned with the curative properties of practice but with the right sort of performance. The shift of emphasis away from 'success' onto 'good practice', can be seen in the training of other occupations engaged in the ambiguous business of therapeutic encounters, such as trainee psychiatrists (Blum and Rosenberg, 1968). Similarly, in the child care teams what constitutes a 'caring relationship' is never a collection of distinct criteria. Good work is not theoretical fluency or a masterful grasp of social work methods but a performance motivated by care and commitment to the consumer. Practitioner conformity to these ideals comes to prominence in the moment of supervision when worker and team leader sit alone together to discuss case practices. In the following interview extract a team leader points to a problem with a worker who is failing to display her adherence to this service ethic. She has detected this in the way that the practitioner's oral account fails to demonstrate that a caring relationship has been struck with the verve and determination expected of a 'good worker':

team leader:	.....some of the team aren't doing the job the way I think it should go. You see some of the team are new and some I know anyway. They're all good workers but you see when I start talking to them I'm beginning to realise that one or two don't know their cases.
researcher:	How do you mean?
team leader:	Well they know who the clients are. They know what they've done with them, they've written up in good style (the records) but they don't seem to show they're really into their clients, into the problem, *going places, committed*, (her emphasis) you know? They are not intending that their relationship will have some impact, er, they seem to be going through the motions.
researcher:	What will you do, er, about the ones you're worried about?
team leader:	I can't tell you which ones, but at this point I'll handle it. What I'll do is talk about the way *I* (her emphasis) would work. How I'd do things you know sort of a model. I'll let her see how I like

things done and then see if there's a
change. If not I'll be a bit more firm...

Some weeks later the: supervisor was asked if she had resolved the problem:

Well frankly (pause) I'm still worried about Helen. Take for
example the Sackman case - you know that one - well in all our
discussions about the case I still can't *see* (her emphasis) the
boy. I don't get the feeling she's got in there, got close to them
- still skating around on the surface, contacting agencies, doing
this and that - quite busy - but not actually getting stuck in. Er,
I've reduced her caseload but it's still not improved. You see
she keeps asking me for confirmation of what she's doing when
really she should be telling me what she's done. Well it's going
to be a learning process, what I don't want to do is undermine
her confidence. I have to keep morale up but point out my ideas
(sighs)....

A week later the team leader quietly mentioned that she and Helen had
enjoyed a long intimate discussion in which the latter revealed personal
problems. These domestic issues are taken by the team leader as the likely
cause of poor performance, however, she will continue to keep an eye on
developments and give more attention to the worker's future oral accounts.
Such accounts, as will be demonstrated later, are largely devoid of
reference to official theories or methods of practice. Instead there is
typically a detailed description of clients and their family relationships that
is bereft of technical jargon. The team leader wishes to 'see' the family in
all their intimate and domestic colour in order to be convinced that the
worker has struck an appropriate relationship:

....as a team leader I have to learn every case, get a picture of
the family, so that if they came into the office I'd almost know
who they were. When they (workers) do that I know they're
getting in there....

This capacity to offer some oral portrait of family life as witnessed or
received, implicitly indicates that the workers are, as the supervisor says,
'getting in there'. They have built a relationship that is 'self evidently'
committed and caring, for it is only by persistence and consideration that
the consumers will be convinced of the dedication of the practitioner.

Consequently the consumers will, it is thought, trustingly impart the intimacies of their domestic lives and in doing so begin to share their problems with the practitioner.

The form and content of oral accounts emerge from the common-sense theorising of members in relation to their collegial and client relationships. The matter of clients and their constitution within oral displays will be explored in later chapters. At this point it need only be noted that the assessment of practice does not relate to distinct criteria surrounding formal skills or methods or the expected outcomes of intervention. Instead, assessment stems from a more circular and complex form of everyday theorising. The workers believe they are engaged in a personalist and beneficial service. Detailed and intimate accounts of family life implicitly articulate this theory and the workers' loyalty to the essential elements of commitment and care. When workers discuss their cases with their supervisor they rarely refer to the official theories of the occupation. Instead, they select cases or aspects of cases to elaborate a shared everyday theory of the necessary and proper nature of their endeavours. Social work is about 'caring' intervention and the detailed description of a particular case is an elaboration of the members' general theory. Likewise, if members are asked to provide a theory of their activities, they assert the general properties of a personalist service through the examples of specific cases and typical problems they face. These examples point to the need for a caring, dedicated practitioner and affirm the rational character of the occupational endeavour. Similar processes have been observed in the counselling services of clergymen. Here Moore (1974) notes how clergymen refer to particular cases as a means of generating a general theory of their practices and a sense of occupational rationality.

Work is 'seen' and assessed as satisfactory in the context of predictive properties contained in oral accounts. Thus it is the very detail of domestic privacies that indicates the worker has now entered the hidden realm of family and individual relationships. Such detail implies a 'good relationship' and this in turn signifies that a satisfactory service is in progress. Other predictive signs also exist when a consumer resists the intrusion of the caring relationship. Here the worker is expected to persist and this also proves her determination, commitment and care for the consumer. Thus within the setting, the test of good work and progress is the practitioner's ability to provide an accumulating picture of domestic relationships throughout the sequence of supervisory encounters. Furthermore, an ability to persist in the face of danger, disappointing rejections and no appreciable results also stands as evidence of the mature and capable practitioner (see Scott, 1969, pp.105-7; Meyer and Rosenblatt, 1975; Heraud, 1981, p.79).

Supervisory encounters: the practitioner's viewpoint

Notions of caring and commitment are a pervasive but rarely defined element of the occupational rationale. They exist diffusely in the displays that members provide about their unobserved activities. It is these symbolic displays that concern us here. However, daily practice is not accomplished simply through 'caring' or being 'committed' but by skilful regard to practical aspects of the occupational experience. Social workers are not simply the incarnation of service sentiments, they may have to be the 'right sort of person' but they are also individuals who wish to regulate their own affairs. In this respect the competent member is able to take into consideration supervisory expectations and her own interests when presenting oral accounts. Through a careful presentation of her unobserved endeavours the worker can win support for her view of events and avoid the discomfort of a more intensive (albeit sensitive) scrutiny of her case practices. This requires the following elaboration.

The team leader cannot plumb the depths of the worker's inner self to gauge her motivational sincerity, she relies instead on a range of linguistic and para-linguistic indications over time. Rhetoric, baptisms of stress and oral exchanges between team leader and worker accumulate into an identity signifying the practitioner's status as a capable worker; the 'right' type of person. This supervisory relationship is however the managed accomplishment of both worker and supervisor, both engaged in an artful balance of access and privacy that protects their respective self-images. The supervisor wishes to assess practice and delicately advise: the team member wishes to be seen as capable and enjoy the comforts of the self-regulating practitioner. Both attempt to manage their occupational interests within this subtle dance of supervisory relationships. Through their knowledge about the other and their own requirements they carefully manage any information which might undermine or offend cherished identities and interests.

There is an enduring tension between membership of a collegial group that stresses the special qualities of the practitioner as one who 'cares' and 'gives', and the requirements of individual comfort and control: This has been briefly noted in social work literature. For example, Syson (1981, pp.141-2) notes the possibility of manipulated accounts given to supervisors by trainees. She makes no elaboration of these incidents but it is apparent from a sociological reading that the students are 'learning the ropes'. That is, they are becoming aware of the discretionary opportunities to fend off unwanted enquiry into their unobserved activities. Similar tactics of concealing or manipulating information to manage disagreeable supervisors has been noted among American trainees (Rosenblatt and Meyer, 1975).

This discretionary or manipulative component of supervisory relationships is a constant feature of social organisation in welfare settings. However, the occupation has largely viewed the issue as a matter of practitioner idiosyncrasy or faulty socialisation rather than a further instance of the negotiable nature of welfare work. In the area office the practitioners display their unobserved interventions through selective and deftly focused oral accounts. While the workers hold their team leaders in genuine regard, they still wish to preserve their own status as self-regulating practitioners. They tailor their accounts to gain advice and support for their view of case circumstances and are aware of items that might invoke a closer gaze. The interview extracts below indicate that the competent member skilfully presents what she wishes to discuss and carefully responds to the enquiries and probes of the supervisor. Both have 'assessed' the other over time and employ their respective knowledge of the expectations and interests involved. This supervisory 'dance' is aptly described as follows:

child care worker: You see I really supervise Louise (team leader), it's in the nature of the job - I only give people information that I want them to know therefore they only tell me on the basis of what I tell them! Yes? Consequently I select what I want them to hear and so get told what I want to hear. To a certain degree therefore I'm hardly likely to be supervised if I don't ask for it....

researcher: What about major decisions?

child care worker: I mean I consult my team leader if I'm making a big change in one of my cases. I also consult colleagues as well, but, er, supervision (pauses) I run that completely....(pause).... though one might say I'm avoiding certain areas, er, but I select what areas to talk about and Louise selects what she wants to hear about - basically keeping each other informed. And in the cases there's a small bit of Louise and her way of doing things and the main bit's me....

The assessment of work occurs within this negotiable process. While the participants agree on the basic parameters of satisfactory work (problem solving in the context of family relationships) their respective interests may not be entirely congruent. The workers in both teams described their adroit management of supervisory encounters in order to sustain their self-image of capable and independent practitioner. They do this on the basis of what they know of the team leader and hence they are aware of the issues that might raise her curiosity:

child care worker   Supervision? (pauses) It's really like a client tells you what they want you to hear and I think I do that. You see you get to know your supervisor and the way their mind works. So if you think their mind reacts in a certain way you don't tell about that...in a way you use it to your advantage really, in a way it's quite manipulative....

Thus, the process of supervision is never a simple matter of matching performance against criteria. Instead it is an unfolding relationship between participants to an interactive career that gradually reveals the identity and skills of both parties. Within this sphere of emergent and affective collegial relationships there are complex dependencies and individual interests to be managed. These are the undercurrents of daily work that lie beneath the constructed harmony of team life:

child care worker: ....we like Joan (team leader), she's a bit of a mother hen and clucks around us like we're her little chicks. But that's nice. But I know her and what she likes and doesn't like (pauses) and I think we're all aware of that in supervision (laughs)....

It is within this close spun web of team affiliations that work is assessed. The supervisory encounter emerges from the variable and temporal distribution of private and shared knowledge, from status conceptions, individual interests and the core assumptions of appropriate practice. It is within these interplaying forms that child care practice is made visible and viewed as satisfactory or otherwise. The good practitioner is committed to a caring involvement with the consumer and this itself is predictive of a satisfactory service. The typically unexplicated shibboleth of care provides a backdrop of rational purpose for the occupational endeavour. While there are occasional doctrinal assertions that practitioners are the really 'caring' members of the organisation and a wider society, it is more typical that practice occurs without explicit reference to the occupational mission of care. Instead, the accounts of unobserved practice are couched in descriptions of family life that implicitly indicate the worker's conformity to service ideals. Her ability to provide a picture of the family, filled with nuance and colour, stands as proof of her caring involvement and a relationship that may succeed in identifying and tackling the problem.

The team leader assesses the practitioner primarily through oral accounts but also through clues and observations gathered over time. The social workers apply similar techniques themselves. Over time they assess the supervisor's skills, expectations and personal characteristics that may influence the way she views appropriate practice. In this respect assessment of unobserved work has to be grasped as a practical activity that is skilfully accomplished by the competent member of the setting. The competent member selects and carefully shapes her account in order to display her conformity to service ideals and win approval for her description of her achievements. She thereby sustains the kudos and comfort of a self-regulating practitioner.

So far there has been an analysis of the negotiable processes that surround the assessment of unobserved practice. The social organisation of work is accomplished within these interactive forms of team membership and supervisory relations. Now it is necessary to investigate the content of accounts in order to complete the analysis. To grasp the content of accounts it is essential to consider first the members' perceptions of the service users. It is only by grasping the typical assumptions and activities surrounding consumer relationships that we may fully appreciate the way accounts are construed and unobserved work made visible.

Ten years later

The two team managers read this chapter with interest and saw much that could be recognised in their own relations with the team and with senior management. Both viewed their role as being accessible to staff as often as possible, both maintained the idea of a 'company of equals' and used the supervisory encounter to deal discreetly with any aspects of performance. They also sought to protect staff from any intrusive gaze from senior managers while they would bring on the performance of a worker to the level required. Management would be approached over worker dereliction rarely and only after other strategies had failed. Performance in relation to expected and well understood standards was searched for during supervision. Also, there were often meetings that were chaired by team managers where individual workers were required to discuss cases in front of families and other professionals. Here, the team manager could witness the way her team communicated with different audiences and could see how well they knew their case. Similarly, team managers would occasionally do a joint visit with a team member when circumstances demanded this and could then observe staff directly. In short, the content of 'good work' and the ways in which this became visible in the work setting had changed and with it some of the assumptions over the purpose of supervision. Everyday work, as we shall see, was much less about family intervention via an ethos of care and commitment, now it seemed more about checking on procedures around child safety. Thus, if child care social work in the late 1990s had become the monitoring of risk in a climate of uncertainty and blame, then so too was supervision about monitoring workers and their adherence to procedures and the avoidance of culpability for worker, team leader and agency in the event of something 'going wrong':

team manager: Reading this chapter it reminded me a lot of the power we had in the old days to decide on our own cases, now we have gone a little too much the other way of being over-constrained by procedures and systems. We are now prone to think about risk and procedure rather than balanced judgement on likely outcomes of doing this or that. It's about systems and safety. Making sure things don't go wrong and if they do that you did things as well as you possibly could. Also, I can be called into court if a worker is away so I have to feel safe too, I need to know pretty well what's going on in the really active cases....

The issue of safety in relation to both child and agency seemed to crop up frequently during interviews with the team managers. Their consequent need to monitor and the object of their monitoring now placed the core topic of supervision some distance from the world observed ten years before. In those days the team leader wanted to know more about the colour and intimacy of family life and the caring relationship struck by the worker with users. Now such detail was quickly summarised en route to what were seen as more compelling issues of what child care was really about, described by both team managers thus:

team manager: There were things in the chapter I picked
                                      up on straightaway, but the one thing
                                      that's gone is the 'care thing'. It's not
                                      about relationships so much and it's not
                                      about power either - we inform families
                                      more, more open than before. But we're
                                      not colluding with them in some cosy
                                      thing. If we had resources I would give
                                      them more. We don't. Now we have a
                                      clearer structure, we're not as woolly as
                                      we were. We all came into social work to
                                      help people, but that's not the game, now
                                      we try to stop kids coming into care. We
                                      work with a small percentage of really
                                      troubled families in a child centred way -
                                      it's the child we focus on. The caring is
                                      still there but it's not some comfortable
                                      or collusive thing....

team manager: Today, you have a relationship of course,
                                      but it's not about being a nice person and
                                      putting things right for the family. It's
                                      about taking responsibility for a piece of
                                      work and that the family understand that.
                                      And if the work is to challenge or protect

114

then the family must know that too. It's not about making their life easier or taking responsibility for them or making them happier. It's about empowering, enabling in a child centred way. I suppose it's a bit like the supervision process - identifying areas to work on to achieve that goal.

Child centred practice defined the essence of good work in the setting, both from the viewpoint of management and most qualified practitioners. Social work assistants and family carers however undertook more of what might be described as 'relationship' work and, as will be seen, had a different kind of supervisory encounter. However, the core work was child safety and its ramifications for staff and agency. Here team managers required a reliable flow of information about events in order to be satisfied that risks were understood and mechanisms in place. This had different consequences for the long term and short term teams. The latter were in the vanguard of investigation and assessment, handing work on to the long term team where appropriate. The nature of work in the short term team seemed to call forth a more interventionist stance which led the team manager, understandably from her viewpoint, to request regular information from the team about case developments:

team manager: By necessity we (qualified staff) are case managers, we don't do direct work so much, we pass that on to family carers. We're a small authority now, with fewer resources and much more rests on what we can do and it will come back to us if things go wrong. So, I like feedback. I like being kept informed. Not everyone does that and that worries me. I don't have as much time as I need for supervision but what I want to see are clear summaries of what they've done, that recording is done, files in order. If they've done an investigation I want to see that other agencies have been involved, that their assessment is clear. For me they have to be able to assess on

115

their feet, say at hospital with aggressive parents, they can keep focused on the child. It might be late at night and with the police there, but they keep level headed and calm despite what's going on around them....

In this hot house world of protection and investigation the cost of getting it wrong can be high. Supervision is a way of driving down the risks of failure. In doing so, checks are routinely made by both team managers on case progress and this is monitored from one supervision session to the next. Here, success would seem to reside more around process and procedure rather than any particular outcome - therapeutic or otherwise:

team manager: I make notes from supervision to check on progress next time - I can tell if they are repeating the story from last time and so I can say 'well what's really been happening here?'. I mean if I hear someone saying 'I popped in and they seem to be OK' then I ask what exactly is going on here. I want clarity. To see things moving on. I also take notes during supervision and give a copy of a brief summary of them to the worker with action points. Basically, I see supervision as monitoring and supportive. I don't see it as me telling them what to do all the time - I give them my ideas and how I would do it from my way of practising - you have to take a child centred approach - there are clear statutory responsibilities. But as far as working a case, I'm open to different types of work with different families provided we don't lose sight of the child and we keep to procedures....

It has to be remembered that the volume and intensity of work in both teams allowed for only the more pressing cases to come to notice in supervision. What was looked for was a clear plan, progress towards specified tasks that would maintain goals around child safety. In such a context, worker-client relationships were seen more as a useful mechanism or conduit for achieving success than any proxy of success itself. Of more concern for the team manager is the child care plan and movement in the agreed direction:

> For me, the absence of a relationship is not itself a failure, a therapeutic relationship will assist, er, you might have to address relationships if staff were failing to develop one in a lot of cases, otherwise I would not be overly worried. What I want to see is something more all round. It becomes evident if they have a clear plan and are moving along it - if there's sound reasoning and they've identified the problem and are dealing with it. I want to see where the child is in all this. If I can't see that then I ask more specific questions, not too bluntly, but I want to be convinced there's a plan there....

As before, shortcomings in performance would be tackled in the quiet seclusion of the supervisory process where team managers would model the way they wished the case to proceed. Most instances could be remedied this way. The examples of dereliction that were cited were not necessarily matters of forming caring relationships but failing to carry out statutory routines, not visiting a child on the child protection register, poor timekeeping, failing to notify the office of whereabouts during the working day. If from this the impression has been gained that supervision is a much more technical and mechanical process than a decade ago then this would be something of an exaggeration insofar as there was genuine warmth and concern by team managers for team members and this was reciprocated by most staff. Mutual concern and support were much in evidence as before. The difference perhaps lay most in the excessive demands on team managers for advice or authorisation given that teams were almost twice the size of those ten years ago. Furthermore, there was an awesome number of meetings for team managers to attend or chair in respect of statutory reviews, core group meetings for children on the child protection register, placement meetings, case conferences. In circumstances such as these, team managers would attempt to pick up details about case progress and related worker performance in contexts other than supervision:

> I sometimes would go on a joint visit but only rarely. I'm more likely to see the team in meetings that I chair - er stat reviews, planning, often with clients there, and I can see then

how well they are on top of the case. I can't go through
every case anyway so I rely on them to tell me. It's like in
your chapter, they still have to tell me the case. And I rely
on honesty between us - so I don't approach things like
'you've got a problem', it's more how can I enable you to
achieve your goals. They're honest with me, I don't think
they're too selective with what they bring, I think I could
detect that....

The team managers generally believed that staff typically shared
information about their cases openly and would not covertly withhold
sensitive material. Given the nature of the work it was indeed likely that
most workers would share their anxieties, their doubts or shortcomings. Yet
they often did so, like those a decade earlier, with a clear eye to winning
approval for their aims rather than diverting the attention of supervisors to
issues that might impede their plan of action. As will be illustrated shortly,
many of the social workers engaged in the careful presentation of their
cases in order to preserve a sense of autonomy over their work, albeit this
work was much more closely bounded by statutory procedures and
administrative regulation than ever existed in the setting of a decade earlier.
    As before, knowledge of the team member gleaned over time in different
contexts gave the team managers an insight into practitioner capacities. In
this regard new work was not paraded in front of the team as a decade
before whereby some recipient was identified in a subtle negotiation
between supervisor and staff. That process of allocating work was long
gone, now, team leaders would during the course of a day give new cases
directly to specific workers as they deemed appropriate. Work allocation
across the two teams was a relatively marginal part of the team managers'
duties, as was supervision, for they were both drawn into a draining round
of chairing or attending statutory and other non-negotiable departmental
meetings. While both team managers had an open door policy for their staff
they were often unavailable because of meetings, or acting as duty manager
for child protection referrals. When in the office, they were frequently
engaged in lengthy ad hoc consultations or catching up on supervision. The
stress caused by these unceasing demands were described with some
emotion by one team manager:

We can't carry on like this. I can't anyway. I'm late for
meetings, cancelled appointments all the time. It's not a matter
of work planning, it is demands. I'm making major decisions
on the stairs, rushing everywhere....It brings out the negative in
me, or I think people see only the negative in me and don't

appreciate that I'm not trying to be in control. But I need information when I need it. My own performance is damaged by all this and I can't help the team like I want to. People don't understand that my role is defined by the need for information. I'm an information manager. A risk manager. I'm far more visible than I'd like to be. I can't be a range of people to the team like in your chapter, it's different now, you can easily get blamed, believe me....

Both team managers shared this view of their work arrangements and relations with their teams:

Your chapter describes the team manager as a 'mother hen', well I'm not the mother hen type. But I do have a brood of chicks who follow me around the office, 'have you got five minutes, have you got two minutes?' They need guidance and advice *now* (speaker's emphasis). It's really difficult to manage (pauses) I feel de-skilled let alone anyone else, I don't have time to bring them on (help and improve staff performance) so quality goes down. I try to deflect it (work pressures) from them but I can't carry it all. I'm not a 'panicker', I don't over react, but the way it is you're forced into making decisions walking down the corridor or on the way to the toilet (pauses). It's the Children Act, local government reorganisation, it's the structure here. Frankly, it feels scary right now....

Much of the work of the team managers stood in stark contrast to the style and focus of supervisory work conducted by the team leaders of the 1980s. This had consequences for the way staff themselves perceived the supervisory encounter both in the context of day to day work and in the quiet moment of supervision. The staff were well aware of the severe demands made upon the emotions, energy and morale of their team managers and were genuinely concerned for their well-being. This however did not make their own occupational needs as practitioners any easier to meet and there was a sense of ambivalence for some over what they saw as an unacceptable level of supervisory interest in their handling of cases. In the world of child centred practice where safety is paramount and where unfair blame is seen as a predictable outcome if, despite best efforts, things go awry, in such a world worker autonomy appeared more uncertain and more contested than a decade ago:

We understand (team manager's) problem, too many staff, no senior practitioner below to delegate to, but (team manager) is not comfortable delegating anyway it seems to me. I think (team manager) wants to have a finger in everything. I can understand some of that but I still jealously guard my independence. There's less time than in your book for supervision. If I make a decision there's a level when you take it to (team manager) and I judge that to an extent. So I get on with my own stuff mostly and I feel generally confident that I will get support for my ideas....

Such viewpoints were likely to be echoed by qualified staff with several years of experience. Nonetheless, they too would construct their encounters in such a way as to protect themselves in the hostile environment they worked in. For example, one qualified and experienced duty worker observed:

I don't think I would withhold anything from the team manager. I share my plan, I still have to work with (team manager's) reservations, it would be dangerous to do otherwise - especially in this blame culture - in the agency and outside....but I feel secure enough in my own work to share, and she's always got an open door, only she's never there or in a meeting. I'm worried about her, she's on overload, she'll burn out, the pressures on her will make her look like she's failing and that would be quite wrong....

This theme was taken up across both teams, by old hands and recent arrivals to the office. One qualified worker who had joined within the last few months observed:

It's not that different to where I was before only more frantic. It's the way it is today....my experience is that supervision here involves an urgency to check the system out, that the process is safe, that children are safe - the children then the agency - it's not devoid of people - but it's the organisation saying the child first. And the team manager is first, as you said, first among equals. But (team manager) is under such strain, we've no substantial resources, so we can't develop, can't learn new things, we stultify and (team manager) knows that and finds it really upsetting....

It was evident that the supervisory response of the short term team manager was different to that of the long term team supervisor; this was not simply due to personal characteristics but to the different operational demands which played upon their management styles. The short term team manager had to police the boundary of the agency particularly in respect of referrals over possible child harm and was often the final arbiter over any organisational response and would be the party for whom the buck stopped if the wrong decision was made. The long term team manager would deal with cases that had already been assessed by the short term team as in need of continuing intervention. While these cases often involved crises there was not the same daily drama as in the short term team over whether some incident or other concerning some hitherto unknown child warranted immediate action. Such differences were well recognised by staff, most of whom also pointed out that the senior manager, who held responsibility for the overall operation of the office, would also get directly involved in the minutiae of case activity on occasion when team managers were away. This point was put clearly by a member of the long term team:

> We have two team managers with very different styles, this has quite an impact on the office. In the long term we tend to have a less intrusive style than in the short term. But you see the short term team have to deal with whatever comes through the door, they have no choice, so (team manager) is perhaps inevitably drawn more into their cases. I wouldn't like that and I think some of the short term team don't find it comfortable. We also have (senior manager) who comes in a lot and is quite hands on, unlike any other manager I have met. In some ways it's good you have two sources of support. But you can also have two different responses from them, so you have to be careful about seeking advice or you could get your plan changed!

This worker, like others, trod a careful line between seeking advice from a manager and retaining some autonomy around a preferred plan of action, while at the same time not exposing herself to risks that might accrue by withholding some aspect or other about a case. This delicate dance between worker and manager over the control of case practice was remarked upon by several respondents from both teams, both qualified and unqualified.

> qualified worker: I get supervised fortnightly and we agree what cases I take on....I am careful about what I select to discuss, you can't help

121

that anyway, but I do want to get their concentration more on some points than others. But you can't afford to be too selective in case something goes wrong. If anything, I tend to talk things up more than they are to get resources, I make things more visible than hidden.

unqualified worker: I'm not going to be questioned quite so much as I'm a family carer - no big decisions - I share as much as I can if I'm asked. But it's like in your chapter, some days it's all rush, some seem to be dashing all the time, and they get as much advice from the staff as anyone. Others keep their heads down and don't offer advice. But I enjoy supervision and I try to make sure my back is covered. I want them (management) to know what's going on so's there's no blame on me....

qualified worker: (names team manager) feels the need to know everything what's going on. What everyone's doing all the time and that's too much for (team manager). to really absorb. And when we have supervision it's often interrupted and then you repeat everything again in passing during the day, constantly giving information. But I do have some space within that to get across what I want, there isn't time to tell everything so it can help you do things your way sometimes....

unqualified worker: I'm a social work assistant, I do more preventive work. I have supervision every couple of weeks, other than that I grab (team manager) when I can. I definitely lead the discussion where I want it to go. I select cases and the issues. I don't feel I'm being assessed in

122

supervision but my case is. But they (cases) don't have priority like the others (qualified staff). But if I've made a mess I say so quickly. I don't have that qualification to protect my point of view....

qualified worker: We're not involved in decisions like we should be. We're more like worker ants bringing back information for managers to decide on, there's little empowerment for me, let alone the client. You see, we are turning from a solution oriented agency to a problem oriented one and I think that stems from the team manager. I think before, like in your chapter, the supervisor would tackle staff problems in a therapeutic way, now it's more about control. Now we don't have weaknesses to be developed but problems to be rectified....

While the form of supervision had not changed overly in the intervening years, the substance had. shifted significantly. The bulk of the direct 'relationship work' delivered by family carers and social work assistants (what a decade ago was viewed in the setting as the core of child care practice) was now the almost exclusive province of unqualified staff who appeared to have less supervision and greater control of their cases than qualified colleagues. The latter, who were more engaged in child protection care management, seemed far more prone to supervisory involvement than was ever evident ten years before, particularly those in the short term team who were in the front line of investigation and assessment. That the everyday work world had become for these social workers a much more legal, technical, administrative and risk reduction activity seemed scarcely in doubt. Yet, there was still the subtle management of information by staff in order to obtain endorsement by managers of some plan or other. Contrariwise, there was also the moderating influence of disclosure as a hedge against blame, an issue that most workers remarked upon. Thus, if the supervisor knew and supported some past or planned action then at least the worker would not be 'alone' when the proverbial fan was hit. Of course, the sheer demands made upon team managers reduced the time they had to supervise workers thereby allowing more opportunity for worker discretion. Yet for many staff there seemed little of the caseload entrepreneurialism that characterised the workers observed in the 1980s. It is to this generation that we now return in order to explore issues of case autonomy and control and how this influenced the client worker relationship.

6 The client: common sense theory and everyday practice

Those who receive welfare services have been referred to here as 'clients', 'consumers', 'service recipients' and so forth. This has been essential to avoid a repetitive use of 'client' which itself is a term that barely denotes the complicated exchange between those who deliver and receive the service. The issue here is not one of a revised term or definition but an investigation of prevailing perceptions that constitute the client as a shared relevance in the office setting. It will be shown that the workers employ their own common-sense theories about those they visit in local communities. This common-sense theory is drawn partly from the formal occupational knowledge base but it also contains the accumulated experience and wisdom of working in the setting itself. Other important tributaries of daily knowledge stem from the worker's membership of a wider community than the colleague group. Indeed it is the case that members of all professions will reflect to some degree the views of the wider laity in relation to their occupational task (Hughes, 1928, p.764).

The competent worker relies on this diversity of knowledge to resolve the uncertainties and dilemmas of practice. For example, the worker may draw on the official virtues of care to justify her activities. She may also apply her specific knowledge of supervisory expectations to provide a suitable account of her work. Similarly, in respect of the client, the worker may rely on her membership of a wider moral collective to grasp the conduct and attitudes of the people she visits. Consequently it should be no surprise to find that the 'client' is understood on the basis of complex knowledge sources containing contradictory elements. Yet this dissonant everyday theory is for all intents and purposes a coherent body of knowledge. It is the basis for 'thinking as usual' (Schutz, 1964, p.95). It will now be shown that the client, as an abstract notion, is revered by the workers. They invoke, as does the formal occupational theory, the client as the object of service. Indeed the client's right to an ethically guided service is clearly encoded (BASW, 1977; CCETSW, 1976) and occupational values proclaim the service-user to be a self-actualising and autonomous individual. Yet the workers are also able to draw on the shared view that clients in 'real life' are often a troublesome and morally deficient type of people. In effect, the workers are able to conjure up both these contrary images in order to understand and resolve certain problems.

This recourse to assessments of moral rectitude would seem to offend the official version of the non-judgmental, empathic practitioner. However, this is by no means peculiar to social work. Other people-processing occupations such as the police (Bittner, 1967) ambulance personnel (Sudnow, 1968; Hughes, 1980) doctors (Strong, 1980) and nurses (Walsh and Elling, 1977) have been observed to make moral distinctions about the worth of their clientele. In brief, there are always opportunities for service providers to judge the social worth of their clients and it is unlikely that professional training will ever inculcate and preserve some moral and uniform neutrality (see Becker *et al.*, 1961, p.323-7).

Within the office, the client may be coated in or stripped of moral rectitude, depending upon the matter at hand. For example, when justifying the need for more resources or some course of action the client may be eulogised and service ideals invoked. Alternatively, when defending themselves against an unmanageable demand on their energies and emotions the workers can apply the shared view of clients as unworthy and in need of close regulation. The source of such views cannot be attributed to some notion of faulty occupational socialisation. Rather, assumptions about clients are steeped in a common-sense theory that arises from the practical experience of doing the job. This theory will now be considered in relation to three areas of practice. These are, the preferred routines of work with clients; the construction of shared understandings about the clientele; the typical ways of managing relationships with clients. In the course of this it will be shown that the abstract, formal meaning of the client as worthy participant in the welfare endeavour is matched by practitioner folk-lore of the client as sometimes venal, unappreciative and in need of careful management.

Welfare rights and welfare rites: preferred work with clients

Welfare rights work; that is, acting as advocate or representative for clients in respect of their financial and material problems, is a familiar feature of the occupational chore. Social workers are frequently engaged in mediating between the client and other state welfare institutions. These activities are commonly referred to as 'welfare rights' work. Yet there are also 'welfare rites'; that is, the accustomed, dignified and prized properties of practice. In the setting it is evident that welfare rights do not fall into this category. It would be useful therefore to pursue briefly those aspects that fall outside the realm of preferred work in order to delineate more closely the boundary of 'proper' practice with clients.

There is little doubt that the child care workers operate with a clientele who are materially disadvantaged. Yet like workers elsewhere (Stevenson and Parsloe, 1978, p.324; Satyamurti, 1981, p.168-175) they view their involvement in welfare rights and financial matters as an undignified departure from their preferred styles of practice. For example, section one of the 1980 Child Care Act gives local authorities the discretionary power to assist financially families in distress. To secure such resources in the office the worker has to gain the permission of both office and higher management. Managerial scrutiny of these applications for finance tilts against the practitioner's preferred image of capable self-directed worker:

> ....if you want money for the client you've got to go and get the OK. That means seeing (office manager) who then asks you all about it and then he may have to get the OK from headquarters (city department). Basically it's a rigmarole. My aim is to make sure they (clients) get their dues from sup-ben (social security). I help them there if it's necessary, but like I say, it's not a big part of our work....

There is also the view that 'money' sullies the relationship between client and worker. Indeed, requests by clients for financial help suggests that they have incorrectly grasped the purpose of child care work and are attempting to impose their definition on a service that practitioners intend to manage and control. The social workers recognise the presence of material deprivation but their inability to do little more than provide occasional and scant relief is rarely a topic of discussion. 'Everyone knows' that the straitened circumstances of countless families are beyond the organisational resources of the office, the department and social services in general. This 'fact' is too obvious to merit comment within the setting and rather than debate the dispiriting issue of material deprivation the workers proceed on the assumption that what they do is beneficial despite these imponderables.

While social workers are not well versed in theories of stratification and material deprivation (Sinfield, 1974, p.72), they are nonetheless aware of the hardships faced by those they visit. They do not engage in callous neglect or blind indifference. Rather, they protect themselves from the inequities they see by asserting the essentially worthy nature of the service they provide. They draw and continually re-draw the boundaries of appropriate work in order to avoid further uncertainties confounding their occupational world:

> child care worker: Most of my clients are what I would call poor, we all work with people who are generally the least well off, we end up with all the problems that other agencies can't cope with, but there's nothing we can do about it! I can't solve poverty, all I can do is work within the family, there are often problems there that lie behind, yes? I don't ignore the fact that they're poor but my work isn't in that area, that's got to be a national or wider political thing....

Social workers do not simply shrug off the presence of deprivation, rather they filter such things out of the daily agenda by immersing themselves in the exigencies of the moment. They are aware of the collective character of structural inequality, they can rise above their cases to see that their attentions centre on predominantly poor families, but they locate the causes and solutions outside their occupational remit. Theirs is the wholesome endeavour of skilled caring relationships; an honourable and worthy tradition that transcends present and future social systems. This sense of mission and distance from the corruption of 'society', and the inherent frailties of human association that will always demand the intervention of skilled practitioners, can be noted in the occupational literature (see Davies 1981, p.208-9). Workers stress the 'eternal' aspects of welfare giving, and one member in particular did not enjoy being asked about the complicating issue of poverty as a potential topic of occupational attention:

> My work is about families, er, child development in families, that's a problem that will be with us forever - there will always be parents and kids who hurt each other and themselves and that's my work. (probe welfare rights and work with poor families). I don't do a lot on the material side, if it's DHSS I throw it back to them (clients). If they don't get where they're going then I intervene if I can. But it's not a big part of my job.

128

I must confess I'm not very big on the old financial side. I pall on that side. I tend to forget people are poor because I'm not very financially oriented myself. If I can get material stuff I do but I don't take a welfare rights view of social work. Don't get me wrong it's not that I don't take a structural view - it's just that welfare rights as my work - I don't get very excited about it, *don't* (her emphasis) press me on that one....

In the setting the more prosaic matters of welfare rights work and other lesser chores related to giving the client practical help are considered suitable for trainee social workers or volunteers and are delegated where possible. This has been noted in the occupation generally (see Abrams, 1980, p.20). There have also been suggestions that welfare rights work and tasks related to the client's financial and material needs could be dealt with by a non-social work staff (see Stevenson, 1981, p.119; Barclay, 1982, p.49). This is a feature of professions generally; those lower down or outside the profession are assigned the less desirable or demeaning occupational tasks (see Hughes, 1958).

This notion of hiving-off the less desirable work or shedding work with less desirable people is a feature of occupations that are seeking to enhance their status (Walsh and Elling, 1977). Working with poverty or the poor is not these practitioners' ideal image or objective and, while they inevitably deal with poor working class families, they nevertheless build their identity around the prized elements of practice. Thus 'real' work in the setting is viewed as a caring, counselling involvement with families. These core properties of the ideal image are built up by the workers as a unique and vaunted element of the job itself. The hallowed traditions of child care mark out a distinctive identity; their work is 'caring', 'demanding' and 'skilled', and most have undergone some occupational baptism of harsh experience. These are the welfare rites that members invoke and all agree that their object of service is the specific realm of family problems.

The workers see themselves as an elite element of the organisation. Their shared rhetoric of stress and hazard marks them off from other colleagues and practices in the office and in the city department. Those engaged with other client groups are considered to be less involved in the traumas and urgencies that child care workers experience. Within the child care teams the workers appeal to the dramatic imagery of their work and consider this experience a positive hallmark of their chosen career:

I chose child care because it's good for my own development as a social worker. It's more demanding, there's statutory duties

129

and that stuff, court work and I couldn't really stand working with the elderly - I mean that's important - but this work is unpredictable and, er, interesting, you learn a lot about yourself....and life....

The idea that workers might receive wisdom, insight and occupational kudos through their interventions with families is part of an occupational exchange that has been only briefly noted in welfare literature (see Titmuss 1973, p.243). However, in the workers' view they 'gave' and perceived few tangible rewards in return. Thus, while child care work itself is seen as the core prestigious segment of the occupation, the clients themselves play scant part in the assembly of this elite identity. On the contrary, they are grasped on the basis of individual and shared experiences, that transform them into a contradictory but coherent reality; an object with generalised properties and characteristics recognisable to the membership. The competent member learns these contrary elements and assumptions and thereby manages the uncertainties and problems of practice. It is towards this occupational identity of the client that the enquiry now moves.

A sort of person: the client as a necessary myth

The notion that clients are seen not as generalised worthy citizens, but a 'sort of people' with substantial negative qualities marking them off from the rest of the public, is rarely explored in the occupational literature. Yet this is a compelling feature of the workers' everyday understanding of the job. Within the setting the client is sometimes cast as unworthy, dangerous and exploitative. The reasons for this have to be grasped in the very experience of work. Practitioners occupy a world where esteem, success, appreciation and creditable technologies are in short supply. Faced with uncertainties the workers do not consign their endeavours to some lowly status but assert the importance of their practices. In doing so they export their occupational shortcomings to those 'outside'. The client is prominently included within the set of guilty others responsible for the dilemmas and frustrations of practice. Occupational failure and uncertainty are resolved by mythologising the client into a collection of contradictory elements that can be selectively invoked in order to manage matters of the moment. The client is both worthy and unworthy; a supernal abstraction and simultaneously a morally defunct and discredited species. These dissonant assumptions become a coherent identity; this, as Manning notes, is the very purpose of myths, they function to:

....arrange themes that are in reality unacceptable or bipolar into integrated or holistic units. (1979b, p.325).

The contradiction of clients being both worthy and unworthy is integrated and made plausible within the occupational experience. The social work mission of commitment and care runs tandem with a seam of practitioner resentment. Social workers face daily an infinite queue of distressed families and in order to ration their skills and efforts they require more than the ethical absolutes of the official occupational dogma. While selfless dedication to the worthy client remains a core virtue, there also remains the mundane world of daily, sad, and sometimes sordid lives to encounter and manage. The occupational failure to do more than 'patch up' this queue of families cannot be the failure of dedicated practitioners; instead it is dramatised as the failure of clients themselves. Blaming the client for their own problems becomes a means of managing occupational impotence and gaining distance from the tragedies and despair they witness. Clients are cast as moral failures, a 'sort of people' that these sorts of things happen to.

Almost any human feature may be described in worthy or pejorative terms (see Cohen *et al.,* 1964). Consequently, the value perspectives that permeate the client-worker transaction can be discerned in the practitioners' very use of the term 'client'. Here, the eulogistic and dyslagistic properties of the term do not tell us about clients as such, but about workers; their attitudes and assumptions. Thus, those pejorative connotations that downgrade the client reinforce the view that workers are morally and, for all practical purposes, the dominant partner in the welfare encounter. Indeed the term 'client' is linked to a discourse of objects that may be negatively rated by this association. For example, when workers describe discreditable aspects of their own occupational behaviour they do so by likening their actions to those of the client. In the extracts below the workers use the phrase 'manipulative'. This term is typically applied to clients who attempt to subvert or exploit the worker's objectives, or to disguise their own conduct and motives. This in turn becomes a practitioner idiom that may also be used to describe questionable aspects of the workers' own conduct:

We're like the clients really, we manipulate, er, you know, write things (in the record) and keep certain things out....

...it's a bit manipulative, er, supervision. You sort of say things in such a way, er, what they want to hear, it's like the clients with us....

I'm like a client really. I manipulate other agencies to get what
I want, but then it's for the client do you see?

Within the occupational literature there have been suggestions that those
social workers who withdraw their affect from consumers and attempt to
distance themselves from the emotional problems they witness are, in
effect, behaving 'like clients' (see Mattinson and Sinclair, 1979, p.265-7).
In short, to be 'like a client' is to act with dubious moral purpose. The
significance of these observations is not to point up practitioner foibles but
to indicate that the 'client' is typically viewed as a diffuse problem species.
They become a 'sort of people', daily constituted within an enduring and
emergent folk-lore that provides workers with an abundant source of
wisdom and precedents to resolve the issues at hand.

Other occupations dealing with the public, such as the police, feel
polluted by their contact with a population they come to see as incorrigible
and unappreciative (Manning, 1979a, p.108; 1979b, p.314). Similar
responses can be discerned among the child care workers who believe they
are faced with a burgeoning and draining clientele. They speak of the need
for physical and social space between themselves and the twilight world of
families on run down council estates and the tightly packed terraced homes
of the dock and sea-front areas they visit. The workers also allude to a
threatening universe of potential clients in the localities they visit. This
adds to their sense of isolation and drama, and demonstrates to all
concerned the need to ration and closely manage their own time and
energies, in order to cope with these 'sort of people'. Clients then are cast
as a problem-species and understood in the following assumptions shared
by the practitioners.

The culture of clients: a problem-species

Practitioners do not spend their day debating 'what is a client?'. Rather,
they address the problems of the moment on the basis of tacit, rarely
articulated assumptions about the families they visit. The client is
consigned to the background of perception as 'everyone knows' what a
client is. Everyone knows that in the abstract they are the treasured objects
of service. Everyone knows they are also the trying and traumatic source of
daily occupational discomforts. The contradiction does not usually jar;
instead the competent member adroitly negotiates these aspects and
situationally invokes the salient side of the client image.

Occasionally, the worker experiences moments that bring the
accustomed background context of client relationships to the foreground.

132

For example, workers spoke of meeting clients outside of working hours and in social contexts other than office or home interviews. Their resulting sense of vulnerability and discomfort indicates the highly structured nature of client relationships and the tightly drawn boundaries of client and worker identities. The following conversation between two team mates points up this experience:

....you've got to be honest you know I prefer to live out a bit, it's no fun to meet your clients in your own time. They want to know when they'll see you again - you know - and frankly in my own time I don't want problems.

Yes you're right, I was at the (local night-club) the other night and I saw Mr. Pearce. It was funny, we didn't say anything. I was glad in a way, but you're right it's funny, specially in a club when you're drinking and relaxing and dancing....

Other workers joined the conversation and shared accounts of being 'caught out' in shops, pubs, and places where the occupational personas of both parties are structurally unlocated. These moments of incongruity occur because they are outside of the bounded and subtly ruled normal run of interaction. The sense of unease stems from the inadvertent display of a private rather than the carefully constructed official presentation of self. It is through this 'self' that the client is managed and maintained at a distance. Distance is essential because there is the shared collegial assumption that clients are all too often devouring, instrumental and unappreciative. Hence it is crucial to maintain an occupational mask that takes cognisance of the following collegial viewpoint expressed at a team meeting:

| child care worker: | It's a funny thing to say but the people around here are cold, in a way you get the feeling they're very instrumental. |
| child care worker: | Yes, they're sort of 'clever pants', er, hard sort of people, it might be the dock life, but yes you do get that feeling.... |

This observation was explored more fully when workers were interviewed about the people they regularly visit and the localities in which they live. The responses typically referred to poor housing and other material deprivations, together with a view of the clientele as a potentially overwhelming and predatory threat:

> ....God! Well if it wasn't for the fact that I have normal friends with normal problems you might think that the whole of this area was one big problem, em, it obviously isn't, we only see one small percentage, but that's still the tip of the iceberg that we don't get round to seeing....

The clientele are viewed as members of a large community of potential clients; a universe 'out there', threateningly close and requiring careful management:

> I would say that I don't like the people round here, and I would say that's a general opinion here. You feel they are sharp, they're toughies, it's the docks probably, but you feel you have to keep an eye on them, that they're after something. It's a strange feeling but I've heard other people say this, but you feel sort of alienated from them...

Like social workers elsewhere (Phillimore, 1981, p.46) the workers spoke of their difficulties in engaging the co-operation of male members of the family particularly fathers and husbands, and of necessity spending more time with the female members:

> I don't like (local) people, I genuinely don't like them. I find the men, er, a lot of macho about the men - the men are arrogant, very opinionated....I don't deal with the men in a lot of cases, mainly with the wives, but that's often the case in any area, as men are less susceptible to social work....

This shared notion of being surrounded by a sea of disagreeable people, stands in stark contrast to the official social work view of the 'community' as a potential source of informal care and affection. The idea of neighbourhoods in need of agitation by workers to awaken the dormant or disorganised sources of local altruism has been a persistent theme of the occupational imagination. There have been, however, cautioning voices that 'community' was born of a past necessity to defend against collective hardships and is now something of a nostalgic illusion (see Abrams, 1980, p.19; Pinker, 1982a, p.70; 1982b, p.241; Pearson, 1983, p.82). This view has never outweighed the optimistic version of the caring community lodged in the official social work viewpoint. Yet, within the occupational literature, there has never been the suggestion that workers might hold an entirely contrary perception of the 'community'; one that casts the inhabitants as distinctly pathogenic, threateningly numerous and hostile to the occupational mission.

The child care workers do not view their clientele as 'working class' or 'poor', rather they are a specific 'sort of people' who have departed from the practitioners' expectations of appropriate family life. The clients are generally cast as a diffuse problem-species. Their departure from the values of the 'respectable' majority is evident in their attitudes and conduct, marking them out as members of a particular cultural universe. This universe is socially and geographically distinct and is seen by workers as a unique population in need of their special attention. The idea that the clients are substantially different from the rest of the citizenry is a necessary assumption that legitimates the occupational endeavour. The search for distinctive properties of a client universe is a feature of most agencies of social control (education, police, health, welfare). They legitimate their activities by calculating a realm of unmet need around a special clientele set apart from everyone else:

> In the course of defining and clarifying the universe which they claim needs their services, all control agencies in effect become responsible for drawing clearer lines than in fact exist either in everyday life or in the procedures by which people were originally led into their services, and agencies may come to define people as deviants who would not originally have been so defined. (Freidson, 1977, p.399-340).

The workers draw such boundaries around their clients and around the areas in which they live. The workers postulate a distinct realm of threatening, disagreeable people who can only be dealt with on the basis of carefully managed encounters. The notion of the voracious, instrumental client forever hovering in large numbers in the wings of the occupational stage is a dramatised projection held by several of the child care workers. However, practitioners occasionally recognise that they exaggerate the size of this ominous universe:

> ....me and Marion were talking about an estate (municipal housing) and a student nearby probably thought we were condemning all the people there. You see they (clients) are a minority on the estate and not all our clients are the same. I

suppose we were quite glib really because it doesn't look good to students to see us being judgmental. As it happens we all say this and that about clients, but they're the minority. But you get cheesed off in this job. Our job is problems and you get to saturation point - you switch off....

Like other workers in service organisations, the collegial group create their own local orientations towards the clientele (see Blau and Scott, 1963, p.84-5). By emphasising the burdensome character of the clientele they justify their right to practice and display their occupational worth (Roth, 1972, p.850-1). That workers do stylise and emphasise the client as a negative property can be discerned in the instance of the 'exceptional client' (see Blau and Scott, 1963, p.84-5). Here the atypicality of a client stands in sharp distinction to the routine assumptions about service recipients:

....Tony's a sweetie, he's different from most of them I'm supervising, he's really not a thug, well I've seen no signs....

....it's so nice to find someone who doesn't know the system (i.e., seeking only financial or material support from the worker)....

....this boy's unusual really, he's not run of the mill. University material I think....

The assumptions of the client as an exploitative and unworthy recipient reinforce the shared image of practitioners as case-hardened experts who really 'know' what work is all about. They learn that they have no secure technologies to deal with the unending queue of family problems that come to the office. Unpredictability and uncertainty characterise their interventions. In an effort to make sense of this, workers create and invoke the profane identity of the clientele, a 'sort of people', instrumental and manipulative. A host of negative attributes bears witness to clients' failures rather than any shortcomings in the service the workers provide. While they believe themselves to be dedicated and motivated by care, they often pass ironic comments on their service ideals and ethics. Workers also, on occasion, mimic and caricature clients. This helps defuse anxieties (see Emerson, 1969) and helps in distancing the worker from the frequently recalcitrant and painful problems they encounter. Most occupations and relationships contain this 'backstage' or unobserved region where insiders engage in comments or conduct that are inconsistent with the expected image (Goffman, 1971, p.71). Indeed, to engage in the negative lore and myth surrounding the clientele signifies the worker's membership of this elite band of child care veterans.

Arms length: normative distance in the welfare relationship

Within the occupational literature it is not difficult to secure contrary versions of the occupational purpose. While the orthodox view is one of a caring profession, there are alternative notions of the social worker as agent of class interests. Here the worker is cast as assiduously supervising an unruly proletariat. Yet, this notion of the 'coercive social worker' scarcely fits the daily world of workers in the office. Here the practitioners are much more concerned to ration or refuse the demands made upon their time, skills and emotions. Like other social workers (Sainsbury, 1975, p.85; Satyamurti, 1981, p.145) they individually and collectively spoke of their reluctance to remove children from families or to exercise their considerable statutory powers. Seeking a care order in court, albeit a rare event, is viewed by the team members as a daunting prospect. Similarly, the relatively few cases of non-accidental injury to children are dreaded and seen as traumatic for all concerned. Like other social workers (Giller and Morris, 1978) they much prefer to win the assent and co-operation of those they visit. To this end, they seek to present themselves to clients as capable and concerned yet sufficiently distanced and formal in order to control the pace and direction of the relationship. While workers define their relationship as 'caring' it is also a subtle but firmly managed affair; an art of skilful self-presentation that balances an affective and official identity. In short they create a sense of normative distance between themselves and the clientele. That is, a set of expectations and status requirements that make sense of the welfare encounter. This aspect of their relationships cannot be grasped simply by reference to the conventional notions of a casework guided relationship.

The workers are not convinced of the efficacy of their casework technology and this doubt is shared by other workers and social work educationalists (see Satyamurti, 1981, p.186; Sainsbury, 1980, p.13; Goldberg and Fruin, 1976, p.14). They do however state that their interventions are informed by aspects of the casework traditions such as an empathic, non-judgmental style of presentation that encourages the clients to explore their problems. However, all state they typically avoid a deeply searching encounter that may unearth more than they have time to resolve. They believe they have neither the time nor the resources to do more than 'patch up' the fractures of family life. Workers would emphasise this point by confirming that a majority of their cases have been 'on the books' for several years and with no appreciable signs of improvement. This lack of a well defined technology engenders a seam of uncertainty that is managed by the workers through shared assumptions about the moral worth of the clients. On the basis of these assumptions the workers justify their view that the consumers are to be instructed in the requisite statuses, identities and expectations surrounding the welfare relationship. Within this process normative distance is created and continually managed for the following reasons.

The workers, like others (see Blech, 1981, p.25), consider that clients are not always able to appreciate the service nor the worker's need to ration her time and resources in relation to other demands. Client attempts to win more time or criticise the service are often dismissed as immature machinations and evidence of the 'manipulative' tendencies of these 'sort of people'. As Roth (1968, p.47) notes, the 'expert' in a relationship that cannot easily be standardised or measured must justify his or her activities against the claims of other participants to an uncertain exchange. In short, the workers impose their own timetable of routines and relationships in order to resolve their occupational dilemmas. One means of expressing their control is to rule out the strategies and demands of the client by applying the shared negative assumptions surrounding the clientele:

> ....I'd be interested to know what they (clients) thought of my work but mind you, take the Simpsons, you know that one. I had a local councillor (elected member of the local authority) ring me the other day about the daughter. Mum had complained that we weren't doing anything about her daughter sleeping with her boyfriend. Mum says I'm not firm enough and behind my back calls me all the names under the sun. Her opinion about me and my work is not worth the time it takes her to speak - I'm not putting her down, as a person she makes a valuable contribution to that family but her opinion of me is absolute rubbish. With that family if you don't give them what they want then you're 'useless'....(shrugs)....

Client viewpoints may be discredited by reference to their lay status and moral turpitude. For example, clients who criticise past workers in front of the present practitioner are deemed to be playing a 'game' of 'manipulation'. Their opinions are never submitted in the written record or shared with colleagues, unless to demonstrate the inappropriate behaviour and gambit of the client and the appropriate conduct of the worker:

> It's hard to say what the clients think of the service. They won't tell you direct - they sometimes say about workers before - they play it like - 'what a rotten social worker they had' - so you try to be better. Or else they say how marvellous the other one was so you feel you've got to do extra again to get your feet under the table. It's very clever! (laughs). And you know damn well so you don't take any notice of it....

Like other people-processing occupations such as the police (Westley, 1970, p.110-118) the workers establish an in-group solidarity in order to assert their shared sense of esteem. Consequently they do not damage this image by sharing or supporting client opinions that would have a divisive impact on the membership:

> The clients often tell you how they were treated by the last social worker, some would say useless, some would say great or whatever. I feed back if they say 'great' but not the 'awful' unless I thought that negative criticism reflected positively on that worker.....

The client's view is reinterpreted as part of the 'problem'. Angry or damaging comments are managed in the inherently negotiable world of social work. Thus negative comments by clients are 'proof' that the worker is having some impact and this can only be for the best:

> ....you work with clients to meet their needs which they may or may not recognise. What they want and what is good for them are two different things. The client because of their inadequacy wants to be mothered, done for. But you may see it in their best interests to be helped towards independence which is hard for them and they don't like it. Er, in five years time you can say 'you look back five years ago I didn't mother you then, I said go and do it yourself!' OK, up to a point they can come in on it but really it's me saying I know better than the client - that's my job! Surely it's up to me as a social worker to know that person, see what their needs are and try and sort it out! They may not like it - even if they hate me as a social worker I can still be helping them....

Clients have little if any recourse to independent adjudication of their grievances (Ruzek, 1973, p.138-140). While the occupation has debated the need for such a forum (Barclay, 1982, p.191) criticism remains largely a symptom of the 'problem' and a moment of therapeutic potential for the practitioner to exploit (see Scott, 1969, p.126; Nurse, 1973). In brief, the client like others in service organisations (Goffman, 1952, p.451-3) is 'cooled out' and viewed as generally ill-placed to judge the quality and objectives of the occupational endeavour. While these assumptions permeate the welfare relationship it would be quite wrong to assume that workers conduct themselves with strident and forceful authority. Instead, they secure their control of the relationships through a delicate balance of affective concern and formal distance. While educationalists have sought to capture this relationship in the abstract notion of a 'disinterested love' (see Tillich, 1969) this scarcely denotes the complexity of assumptions and practical manoeuvres that produce daily practice. For example, for workers to gain access to domestic privacies they must apply more than a degree of affective concern; they must also engage in the skilful control of information. Like the health service workers observed by Glaser and Strauss (1965) the practitioners engage in 'closed awareness' contexts; that is, they carefully restrict the communication of their assumptions, diagnoses and attitudes when in the presence of clients. Clearly, the workers cannot gain access to family life if consumers are aware of practitioners' opinions of their moral worth:

> (Worker talks to student, points to written record) That's how I can best describe the family, of course I don't give that impression when I'm there, who'd want to know they were a reluctant housewife and their house was whiffy....

During individual interviews all workers spoke of their clear resistance to sharing their written records with those they visit. As in other professions such as medicine (Roth, 1964, p.308), diagnoses, plans, suspicions and impressions are never fully shared with the consumers. While practitioners justify this by reference to the client's best interests, the management of information is clearly bound up with issues of their authority and social control of the welfare relationship. Indeed the relationship is replete with subtly managed and rarely researched strategies that secure the worker's command of the actual interactive encounter. Such matters lie at the heart of the welfare exchange and require the following elaboration.

Interactive distance: lessons in social control

Within the setting the workers are neither self-effacing therapists nor are they despotic intruders; they are, primarily, members of an occupation ill-equipped to solve the problems they face. Consequently they construct their own strategies for dealing with the dilemmas they perceive. These, par excellence, are the shifting, negotiable and emergent definitions that permeate the work world and particularly the client. The folk-lore and myth surrounding the clientele lead not so much to a practitioner lust for power but a need for interactive distance, that is, the control of actual contact and conduct in the welfare relationship. This allows the worker to ration her time and skills in relation to the competing demands made upon her.

The workers share the self-conception of dedicated but hard-pressed veterans. They have no effective methods for achieving demonstrable results and so assume the efficacy or necessity of their endeavours. Without clear criteria of practice they cannot easily convince the consumer that a certain course of action will have predictable results. Without a distinctive product, or clear set of mutual obligations leading to a specified outcome, the workers cannot overtly claim a right to determine the relationship. Consequently the workers rely on indirect forms of control to create interactive distance and thereby manage client encounters. In this respect they share similar orientations to the psychiatrists identified by Daniels (1975, p.72); that is, the practitioners do not perceive indirect influence as a form of questionable control but a necessary skill learned through hard experience. Indeed, workers do not believe they are engaged in some disagreeable form of social control. In their view this sort of 'dirty work' is undertaken by other groups such as the police and state benefit agencies, but never in the subtle ploys and tactics the workers use to manage the clients.

The workers perceive a potentially overwhelming and unappreciative clientele who cannot be considered capable participants to the welfare relationship. Like other social workers (Rees, 1978, p.122) they prefer to avoid an aggressive or conflictual encounter and seek a cooperative rapport with the clientele. Not unlike the medical practitioners observed by Davis (1977), the workers keep a tight rein on assessments and assumptions, which, if shared with the client, might lead to unmanageable reactions. The workers' relationships with the clients are essentially secretive ones whereby workers retain information and ward off those circumstances likely to loosen their control of the pace and content of the service provided. Other occupational groups such as teachers do this; they exercise

141

their authority by persuasion and a subtle 'cooling out' that secures their view of service requirements (Becker, 1976; Hammersley, 1976).

In brief the social workers subtly teach a client to be a 'client'; that is, one who receives rather than determines the service. The workers believe they are the ones who should define the style and content of the service and this has been an observed feature of other welfare settings (Emerson and Pollner, 1978). The child care workers in the office frequently assert they are best placed to evaluate the propriety of demands made by their clients:

> worker to student: You'll get to know when you've got to jump and when you can leave things - like Mrs Pearce - she'll be screaming this and that but when you go there a few days later it's all over. You know, like it sounds like a crisis, but this happens every week so you don't drop everything you leave it for a while so as they know you don't work at their beck and call....

Similar sentiments were evident during interviews. Workers believe the capable practitioner is able to judge circumstances because of her familiarity with the case. Here, the idea of the 'routinised emergency' (Hughes, 1951b, p.313-323) applies to this and other service relationships. That is, practitioners routinely deal with problems that other people assume to be a crisis. The worker's calm and distanced response informs the client implicitly that despite the issue at hand theirs is a 'routine' problem. This also impresses upon the client that the worker is in charge and will define the occupational response. However, there are those cases which are new and an unknown quantity. In the absence of an established relationship the worker feels unsure about the appropriate response. She does not yet 'know' the family nor has she firmly implanted the idea that she is the one who decides on the urgency and authenticity of demands upon her services:

> It's the new referrals I don't like - that's the unknown - you've got to respond quickly to those because you haven't sussed out what's what. With your own cases you know what's going on, things might blow but it's not like a new case which takes time....Dad here (pointing to a case record) wants me to visit urgently, his son's in trouble, but he (dad) wouldn't see me for months, so now he's got to learn we don't visit at the drop of a hat.

Here the worker points to the necessary education of the client. The consumers learn that they may well prompt some response by their requests, but they do not control what service they receive, or when and where they receive it. Attempts to do so are ruled exploitative and a symptom of their disorganised individual or family condition.

Child care workers also act as gatekeepers for their colleagues. They share telephones and can be observed to make excuses for nearby team mates who may not wish to converse with the caller. Observing such an instance, a question was put to the worker who fended off the inconvenient caller. She explained that clients could be persistent and to demonstrate this drew on a familiar story of a client who made spectacular attempts to see a particular worker. The extract below is significant not simply because it constitutes a further elaboration of the folk-lore that legitimates the management of clients, but because it nicely points up the image of the client as a vaunted object of the occupation in the same breath. The juxtaposition of these contrary images within a single comment is not 'remarkable', it is simply a rendition of the myth surrounding clients. That is, the negotiable common-sense identity that workers construct in order to resolve the day to day dilemmas and uncertainties, while retaining a sense of worthy purpose:

....you get to know peoples' cases, like the difficult ones, and like today I know that Joan's got a lot on and this woman phones regularly, so I give Joan an 'out' - you must have seen people saying 'I'm too busy, tell her I'm out' you know when there's a phone call, or when a client comes into the office people scurry off sometimes! We had one social worker, Meryl, and this woman (client) practically camped outside the office to catch her, she had to use the fire-escape to avoid her, it's true!....After a while they get to learn that you can't come out immediately they phone. Like if someone phones for me I'll say I'll come in a few days if I judge the crisis to be small, and usually by the time I get there it's blown over - they've resolved it themselves....(Respondent continues to discuss staff and resource shortages)....take for example this office, we now close the office between one and two o'clock, the office is shut! What's the client supposed to do? There they are with their problem and we're saying 'sorry it's one o'clock come back in an hour and we'll look at it then!', what happens in that hour? What's the client supposed to do? It's wrong really....

As the extract indicates, the clients may be cast as troublesome and also eulogised in the same breath. Like other service performers (see Ditton, 1977, p.69) the competent member can 'thicken' or 'thin' the service ideals to manage the issues at hand. That is, they can apply insider and cynical knowledge to undermine consumer claims and thereby 'thin' the service imagery. Also as the extract reveals, they can 'thicken' the service imagery when appealing to the worthy nature of their endeavours.

The practitioner's performance: lessons for the client

The social workers do not engage in clumsy, authoritarian encounters with their clientele. Instead they present themselves in a well managed display of gestures, tone of voice, posture and demeanour that impresses upon the client the concerned yet ultimately official basis of their relationship. Impression management has been a noted feature of psychiatric encounters (Scheff, 1968) and in judicial routines dealing with deviancy (Matza, 1976). There has been, however, less attention paid to the dramatis personae of social workers. Yet, they too rehearse a 'self' in their interactions with clients that seek to establish control over immediate and future encounters. Phillimore's (1981, p.37) research into a voluntary welfare agency notes the undoubted significance of the style and manner of the worker as a means of gaining access to the private world of families. Phillimore briefly remarks on the paradox of 'friend but official' which clients perceive. However, he does not pursue this notion of a 'friendly official' as a carefully constructed identity which is continuously redrawn as the relationship proceeds. This has been noted by Roth (1972, p.855) in other service occupations which cannot choose their clientele but have to deal with whatever problems surface. Here, the aspect of time is crucial. Those relationships that are long-term have a tendency to gradual socialisation of the clientele, especially where practitioners wish to avoid or cannot invoke a clear right to control the relationship. Hence there is an emphasis upon surreptitious and subtle control.

Roth's observations succinctly apply to the office setting. Social workers cannot gain access to family privacies and cooperation by a stiffly official or assertive demeanour. Yet they cannot control the relationship on the basis of diffuse friendship. Clients that seek to dilute the official character of intervention by attempting more informal relations are not encouraged by the worker. The practitioners see their formal identity as a protection; a means of combating inappropriate demands and behaviour. This was made evident in a team meeting that included the discussion of a client's inappropriate behaviour in his role of service recipient:

144

child care worker:	He's a difficult man to work with. I've visited him a few times and he's tried to make it more of a social thing. You know, he wants to call me by my first name and he sort of looks at me er....
team leader:	yes, I remember this one. The last worker said the same, he'd call her 'love' and be a bit suggestive, sort of knocked her out of her role, you know - sexually - he sort of defrocks social workers! (team laughs)
child care worker:	Yes he frightens me but I don't show I'm frightened. I'm frightened inside, but I've got to work through him to get to the boy, he's a very difficult man but I'm not getting into some cosy or social thing....

The skilled presentation of self, of not showing 'fear' as in the above extract, is part of the worker's craft. They can also choose to appear more 'official' or, reasonably relaxed with their formal status barely visible in the course of interaction. Workers spoke of their adroit use of body posture and control of conversation using techniques such as gentle probes and the use of silence. In brief, they apply a range of linguistic and para-linguistic skills. These skills, born of experience, add to the other secrets of the trade that shape the client encounter. Such secrets include the confidential information received from other agencies and official records. There are also the private assumptions the worker holds in relation to the family or issue in question and their familiarity with the range of services and resources that may be available. This produces a 'knowledge dilemma' which as Ditton (1977, p.46) notes is common to many service situations. Here the asymmetry of shared knowledge engenders a sense of subtle but confident control in the service provider.

Within this realm of artful control lies another significant indicator that points to the careful management of the welfare relationship. This is the use of names between client and worker. There is more to the meaning of names than their apparent use in everyday encounters (see Cohen et al., 1964). Thus when workers insist on the use of surnames in their meetings with clients this has more to do with issues of subtle control than a concern for a well mannered exchange:

Some clients call me Jean, some Mrs. Collins, it's the way it happens, I'm not funny about that but some clients I make sure never call me Jean....

....how you use yourself is very important, like if you're looking into a battering (child injury), like with Mrs. Price, then you note everything going on, you don't sit back and chat, you sort of sit straight and don't get drawn into an easy-going thing, like with Mrs. Price it still is 'Mrs. Price' and I'm 'Mrs. McKewon', you see?

....some clients need a really professional approach, er, you need distance. But the majority of my clients need a 'let's get together and get to grips with this' approach, in most cases it's christian names - but never friendship - we're not friends and it would be wrong to pretend we are, I can only think of one case where I've been a friend and that was justified in that case....

Most workers respond to the client in an evolving relationship that eschews an entirely official character. Indeed, it is part of the worker's repertoire of interpersonal skills to gauge the point when a client can be managed with an easy and affective contact that will not prejudice the practitioner's authority. For example, social workers, like the police (Manning, 1979b, p.153-4) rarely accept gifts from those they visit, and in the few instances that they do they must be sure there are no ulterior motives or manipulative strategies afoot. It is the workers who see themselves as the altruistic 'givers'; gifts from the client symbolise danger, a seductive Trojan horse intended to shift control towards the client:

....things like presents are tricky, sometimes you see them as real appreciation, but we're not here to accept presents, it's our job, and you have to gently refuse sometimes because you're not family or friend and you've got to avoid being sucked into that.

The notion of 'friendship' is skilfully avoided in the developing client relationship. A small minority of workers see themselves as demonstrably 'official' and the clients as unambiguously 'clients', with no scope for this arrangement to be loosened by more affective encounters:

....I am a social worker, I can't go into a home and let them call me Josie, I like them to call me Mrs. Madden. It doesn't mean I give them less as Mrs. Madden. Not one client calls me Josie and I don't call one client by their first name - I put them all on the same level - er, only one is Glenda, I call her Glenda to get through to her, mother her, she's a bit dim. But she doesn't call me Josie. I'm a social worker and they're a client. I'm sorry but don't let's get away from the reality of the situation. I'm not decrying them or degrading them but they are clients. I don't need christian names to make them grow, I can work with them and make them grow as Mrs. Madden, but not as a friend, in reality they're a client. I'm sorry but you're not being realistic to be a friend....

Workers engage in the production of barriers that allow them to manage and adjust the demands made upon them. The client has to learn that the worker dictates the pace and mode of contact and the worker is adept at providing this instruction. The capable worker acquires the interactive skills and devices of subtle control through the occupational experience. Practitioners are well versed in the art of managing themselves before an endless queue of known and new families. What may be an entirely new experience for the client is an occupational commonplace for the worker. The capable worker is able to identify quickly the sort of 'self' she should present in relation to the situation before her

....we can all play the authority role when we have to. I can switch from nice person to very stiff upper lip if I want, like with adolescents, if they go too far you've got to be directive and firm and then go easy on them. Other times you know, er, there's very inadequate types, mums with five kids who are struggling along. You can't bring in the authority bit even if the kids aren't going to school - they need a shoulder to cry on, an arm around them, you judge the situation, that's part of the job....

The moral absolutes and official methods of social work cannot describe the ploys, tactics and know-how of experienced child care veterans and their adroit presentation of self in daily work. Like all the relationships within the setting the client-worker transaction is emergent and negotiable but it is ultimately bounded by the assumptions that create the client as an occupational reality. I have sought no more than to provide some

147

illustrations of this process, particularly in relation to the well managed identity of the workers and their means of teaching the client the role of recipient rather than participant.

The intention here has been to substantiate the client as an occupational entity and the way in which clients are typically perceived by workers. It would be wrong to assume from this that workers engage in cynical manipulation of a deprived and powerless client audience. The workers, after all, believe their intentions to be honourable and their actions worthy. Only they 'know' what work is like and they justify their daily practices on the basis of shared assumptions about those they visit. At root lies the belief that clients are 'clients'; a distinct and separate species made up of abstract virtues and specifically disagreeable elements. Myth and lore validate daily practice and link the client to a discourse of contrary sentiments; The worker is able to draw flexibly on these images in order to reveal her unobserved endeavours and thereby display her competent membership of the setting. This chapter has attempted to reveal crucial properties of the complex and contradictory client identity. The next chapter will set out the oral accounts shared between worker and supervisor that make visible the unobserved encounter with the clients. The full import of these accounts for participants, observer and reader, cannot be grasped without an understanding of the 'client' as outlined above.

Ten years on

The client as a negotiable construct that could be eulogised in abstract or viewed as unworthy for more practical purposes, appeared less evident some ten or so years later. There were two reasons for this advanced by the practitioners. One was the impact on practice of anti-discriminatory training and thereby the possibility that workers had internalised a more positive and unified concept of client as worthy. Linked to this was the self regulatory nature of the colleague group and their readiness to rebuke or challenge their peers over any inappropriate comment about the clientele. Secondly, the notion of working in partnership with clients, together with a more open approach to information and decision making, had made significant inroads into any assumption that service users were expected to be biddable recipients of welfare.

Such changes were broadly welcomed by the respondents yet they also recognised that the warm and persuasive notion of user involvement had, for them, arrived at a period when child care was far more defined by intervention around suspected or actual harm to a child. For this later generation of workers, the challenge was in maintaining ideals around partnership in the context of dealing with crisis, distressed children and angry or frightened parents. Here, however, lay some clear similarities with a decade or more before. That is, many respondents spoke of the families and communities they visited as being intrinsically problematic and likely to be the source of tense relations and in need of careful management, albeit in as open a way as possible:

child care worker:	I've been working here for years and I think clients are more aggressive now. Like in the book, they will sometimes slag off the old social worker to the new one in the hope that you will do more. I think most of us see ourselves as a friendly official, or would like to. I'd say we're all into empowerment, involvement, and this means you have to be very clear about what you can offer when you're dealing with harm, you know, who are you supposed to be empowering? It's a bit of a conundrum. I've been doing duty for some time now and I would say I'm quite critical of the local culture in this town. That doesn't mean I behave differently with people. But I don't live here and most of us don't....
child care worker:	Half the people (clients) I work with hate me, see me as the devil incarnate. But that's often the nature of short term work, you're there at the point some crisis has occurred and you've got the dirty work to do. I need to protect myself in this work, I mean I'm not particularly friendly at first. I don't get very optimistic about outcomes - so I don't try to form close relationships in the first few meetings - that sees me through until I can judge what's happening....

149

child care worker:	I've only worked with the Children Act. What I do know from my time in the long term team is that you can't reconcile child centred and family support. We work with split personalities, we split off our preventative responsibilities. Long term is more about crisis management and monitoring, not family support....the town is quite a rough place to work and we only see a small part of it. But, at least there is an openness to what we do, knowledge is power and the lack of openness that you could see before in your chapter is alien to me....

The view of workers towards the town and the families they visited did to some extent reflect their own location in the setting as qualified or unqualified staff. The latter were typically engaged in what might be described as support work involving home visiting, advising parents, checking on children, and generally engaging in a more diffuse relationship around family care. The qualified staff to varying degrees were more involved in managing child protection procedures and allied processes and this seemed more likely to define how they saw users and communities. For example one unqualified worker observed:

> I think families tend to welcome me more than social workers. I go into houses to do preventative stuff. You make it clear you will report and share what you see. I go in for about an hour, work with children, advise on money, I listen, I don't do anything therapeutic but I do work in an empathic way. I also see children on their own. I've visited with some social workers and I think some are genuinely threatened by some families, I can see that. And some others I think they (social workers) just don't understand what it's like to be these families - you know, where they're (families) coming from....

Another unqualified worker made a similar comment:

> You have to build that relationship to do the better work. We still all believe in caring, but the short term team don't have

150

time for this type of work, I think the long term team do more caring stuff but it's often protection work there too....

It is essential to grasp the core project for most qualified staff which was doing visits to investigate suspected harm and to follow up on cases that arose in consequence of this. In this respect the short term team did fairly quick assessments in order to inform a plan of action. Assessments, as some lengthy court-requested activity entailing observation over weeks or months, was not usually undertaken by the short term team. Also, due to their becoming part of a much smaller authority there was now no access as before to a specialist unit that could offer such a service. On the relatively few occasions that such full and detailed assessments were needed it was the long term team that would do this. The bulk of the work for both teams was much more around checking on a child's safety and making a judgement about where that child should reside and what support might be needed in the immediate to medium term. This should not suggest that workers were somehow indifferent to caring relationships, on the contrary most talked of the importance of establishing an effective rapport with clients, but this was not an aim in itself but more a means to collect or communicate information. If time presented itself, as it rarely did, then direct work would be undertaken that had a more therapeutic orientation. Unlike ten years before, at the heart of practice lay the fact that now the client was the child and not the family:

The Children Act is a major factor in how we work. We explore ways to sustain the family, using extended family for placements, and if we have time to do more direct work with children we do. We're much more aware of long term abuse and how to interfere with that pattern, generally we would refer to a post trauma counselling service. We used to do comprehensive assessments - good potential for direct work - orange book stuff - but we don't have time for that now. Our family carers now do most of the direct work. Sometimes we might work with the child, you see the child is the client and you're there for them. I read your chapter. I can see a lot of what we do there, but in those days we would provide lots of material stuff but we wouldn't always challenge what was going on and how to stop the risk situation. Finance and practical help didn't always help to get near that....

151

Child centred work and the child as the client was now the broadly accepted principle of practice. The concern for risk and the focus upon safety would inevitably place most workers in conflict with some parents at some time. Yet the workers were always concerned to offer as much openness and participation as circumstances would allow. These different interests seemed to collide on occasion as one short term worker noted:

> It's right that we should be challenged and questioned by people. That's absolutely right - I believe that - most of us do. We're pretty solid on values around here. I've been here since 1987 and one of our big changes is with relationships with families. I would not recognise case conferences of ten years ago. Now, families are there, no whispering behind their backs, we're open and honest with them, it's the only way. They need to know exactly what we're talking about. It's much healthier now. But that does mean that people are more able to express their anger, more opportunity to push their viewpoint, and this means that openness can encourage conflict. Can't avoid it in a way....

Most workers spoke of parents as tending to be aggressive and uncooperative, most saw the client as the child, and nearly all viewed the communities they visited as hostile in some way and likely to impede their interest in gathering information about some child or other:

child care worker: It's not the relationship I have with a client that is discussed in supervision but have we done this or that check. Your chapter with a team leader saying something about I want you to paint me a picture of the family, well that was completely unknown to me. I just get facts across. We can only operate on facts. People might want to know what the child is feeling, but if we go to court they will want facts. There is a relationship, that is central to what we do, we validate people's feelings with the relationship. But our aim is to get beyond that. We need to know why people function, yes? But we need to get beyond

152

that to ensure if it's (family) a safe place for children. My value base is still about people's rights and avoiding any abuse of power. I'm child centred but I try not to ignore adults' needs, but the children are the clients, the family is *not* (speaker's emphasis) the client....

Staff recognised that the nature of the work itself and the desire for openness combined to make it easier for parents to voice their anger or criticism. They saw this as part of the job. Also, most viewed the source of many of their occupational troubles as stemming from the impoverishment existing in several housing estates they visited in the town and dockside. Cash support for families living here was available only in exceptional circumstances and rarely featured in the range of services that might be connected. However, staff were able to respond to financial problems by linking families to a welfare rights worker in the department - such a service was not available a decade before. Workers often invoked the vicissitudes of a national and local economy that had long seen the loss of traditional industries and the absence of any significant replacement, as undermining family stability. They described the communities they visited as comprising many families scarred by three generations of unemployment, crime, drug abuse and the slow corrosion of living on subsistence incomes, all of which, in the view of most respondents, led to fragile if not broken families filtering through to the office. At the same time, the well known and unenviable reputation of the town was seen by some workers as an indicator of their own worth as experienced and proven child care professionals:

Sometimes we may say oh my god there's no place as bad as (names town). Maybe it's because we know where all the section one offenders live and so we tend to think the place is full of these characters. The place has always had a bad reputation, highest crime rate. We had an American social worker here who went back to the Bronx and wrote saying that where we work is far worse! But I think we tell that one because it looks good for us, if this is the toughest place then we must be pretty good to handle it! I don't think we dislike the people like some of them did before (points to chapter). It's more in jest, it's a way of saying we must be great to work here....

153

The notion of a threatening universe of families was not unlike before where workers perceived an infinite demand upon the office and themselves personally. That this was still the case was evident in many responses which included reference to the frequent occurrence of verbal abuse and aggression from families. There was for many respondents a sense of weary paradox in the fact that they believed in being more open and honest about their interest in a child's safety. For, in getting this message across they would typically avoid subtle ploys of cooling out the client and be explicit about their intentions. This would expose them more immediately to the hostility of some parents or carers. This was recognised by managers who in keeping faith with a child centred and risk conscious practice viewed relationship work as a means rather than a goal, and a means that could be dispensed with if it meant not facing squarely the overriding question of child safety. This point was succinctly put by one team manager:

> We're more open than those (workers) in your chapter. We're not collusive with them (parents/carers) so we get more verbal aggression. I think the structure is clearer. We co-work with the police and other agencies much more. We are dealing with a small percentage of families who are troublesome, some of these parents are very frightening, very threatening people. Social workers are understandably worried, but we're not going to get comfortable with them. Relationships are important but not some comfortable collusion thing. But the problem is we have no real resource apart from the teams. Not enough foster placements, no specialist therapeutic centre, that (centre) stayed with (neighbouring department) when we had LGR (local government reorganisation). We have very little to tackle some of the extreme emotional behaviour problems we see. People here are angrier and poorer than ever. More violence around. More domestic violence. Women seem more disempowered. There's drugs. There are men who seem to move from family to family. Families often seem to be related in some way through half brothers and sisters. I think most of us would like to find some different way of working with families because what we are doing isn't really providing long term solutions. But this is what we are required to do. (pauses) I'm not sure child care can continue down this road for much longer....

It is difficult to get across the sense of resignation if not exhaustion of this respondent and several others in the setting. While much of the banter

154

about clients and their communities bore some resemblance to an earlier generation, the nature of child care in this setting some ten years on was profoundly different. It appeared far more embattled, more stressful, more interventionist, yet far more conscious of ethical imperatives around anti-discriminatory practice and partnership working. Clients - children and parents - enjoyed a more open relationship but one that sought to gather facts in order to satisfy concern over safety rather than a relationship that might, if time allowed, seek more lasting solutions to family needs. Here, from the supervisor's viewpoint, the 'good practitioner' was one who did not collude with belligerent parents who resisted investigation or denied some culpability. The 'collusive worker' and the 'aggressive parent' had, in their different ways, come to be the source of much anxiety for managers and practitioners in what was now a tough minded business of protection for child, agency and worker. This was the new order of the late 1990s.

7 Telling the case: social work made visible

A generic feature of interaction is the way in which members of a group construct verbal exchanges that not only sustain action but affirm the symbolic structure of the group or membership (Becker, 1972, p.102). This is no more prominent than in professional settings. Here, the idea that good work is displayed through a good account is a pervasive feature of many occupational groups. For example, the hospital ward round (Arluke, 1977) and the hospital casualty department (Hughes, 1977) involve oral traditions that the participant must master in order to be seen as a competent member. These rhetorical features of occupational practice have been observed among court personnel (Carlen, 1976, p.102-3) and in the presentations of expert witnesses, such as psychiatrists in juvenile court (Emerson, 1969, pp.249-267). In short 'speaking on behalf' of a clientele is a key activity of people processing occupations. Yet, relatively little attention has been paid to the varying contexts in which oral claims to an occupational competence occur. This is certainly so in relation to social work. However, this chapter now seeks to demonstrate the broad processes that constitute rhetorical presentation in a welfare setting, with a specific regard to supervisory encounters.

Telling the case, that is, providing oral accounts about clients, is a routine but crucial event in the way that work is socially organised and made visible. It is here in the supervisory encounter, when the worker talks about her cases, that she implicitly affirms her own identity and that of the clients. In doing so she draws on shared assumptions about doing social work in this particular setting and it is in this context that work is made visible and seen as satisfactory or otherwise.

Telling the case: practical reasoning and interpretative procedures

In order to demonstrate the complex elements that make up the supervisory encounter it will be necessary to submit taped verbatim extracts of case talk between team leaders and social workers. These taped interviews could only be gained with the cooperation and trust of the participants concerned. This was possible not simply because of a technically successful research relationship but because the office members were convinced that the research sought to understand rather than impugn their activities. This point needs emphasising because it is not the purpose of this enquiry to discredit people at work or the relationships they construct. Instead the aim throughout has been to reveal the social theories of everyday actors in an occupational setting and the way they order their lives.

The interview extracts that follow are necessarily a minor selection of taped supervisory discussions about young people living at home with their families, but subject to a statutory relationship (care order, supervision order) with the social services department. They have been selected because they highlight both the variety and typicality of oral accounts. Thus while accounts vary in length, detail, tone and descriptive complexity, they all share core properties that create a distinctive oral tradition. This will be introduced shortly. First it is essential to situate case talk in a theoretical context that will complement observations made in previous chapters. This will entail some brief references to particular ethnomethodological concepts. These concepts describe how people assign common-sense terms to everyday objects and events and make sense of their routine social world. However, there will be no thoroughgoing analysis of conversational forms here. Instead, I wish to introduce general properties of the way everyday talk is constructed in order to show that social workers, like all of us, account for themselves on the basis of a shared oral tradition, informed by tacit rarely articulated assumptions about people and objects in the day to day world.

The ethnomethodological tradition insists that social order does not stem from formal rules or norms but from the way these are interpreted by members of the social group. In brief, a sense of social structure is created by people in the way they apply interpretative procedures to the world around them. Manning (1971) employs this notion of interpretative procedures in his analysis of occupational settings. He observes that members of organisations are seen as competent by mastering the oral traditions that make sense of work. This is not a question of learning the formal rules but of grasping the contextual rules of interpretation. Thus, over time, the member learns that various activities can be inferred from formal rules; that the rules may be ironised and glossed over in order to accomplish the practical problems at hand. The competent participant in the organisation understands these shared interpretative procedures.

This approach to a welfare setting has been used by Wieder (1974). He observed how the staff constructed an oral code of their own in order to make sense of their day to day experiences. This code was not comprised of the formal rules of the organisation but was a member-constructed set of interpretative procedures that guided their perception about particular people and problems. In this sense the code was a collection of embedded instructions that had its base in the everyday world of practice. By learning and telling this code or oral tradition the worker makes sense of occupational practices and indicates that he or she is a competent member in that setting.

Within the area office the workers tell the case to their supervisor. When they do this they do not act out formal roles or official rules, rather they engage in the common-sense discourse of habitués, that is drawn from their own association and relationships. In brief, talk has to be grasped in its location of a particular group of people solving their daily problems.

Social workers, like all of us, must establish the bases for their activities. They routinely do so through the medium of talk. They, like most of us, are not professional theorists of the social structure, nor for that matter of the psychological structure of group and individual processes. In this respect their oral traditions are typically bereft of a technical or medical vocabulism. They do not employ some arcane argot; like most of us they live in a broader collective than the work setting. They apply the language of their broader membership to express the common-sense theory of doing social work.

Case talk is nevertheless a skilful process of shared expression that makes sense of everyday life and gives uniformity to people and events. Such talk does not proceed on the basis of indisputable proof to be arrived at by some investigative discourse or 'truth searching'. Nor does talk proceed through the matching of actions and meanings to a readily available and concrete set of rules. Instead talk occurs on the basis of a necessarily self-limiting level of mutual understanding. For example, if our conversations and relationships were really tested against some formal and severe criteria of objective knowledge the result would be confusion. Thus, if greeted with a common-place 'how are you?', a reply that then requested complete clarification of the question (why it was asked and what sort of information specifically was required by way of an answer) would disrupt the typically elliptical and taken for granted nature of ordinary talk (see Garfinkel, 1967, p.53). Thus it is not that we are unable to render our actions to one another in a more analytical style but that typically we do not have to in order to achieve purposeful rational activity. Were we to demand the application of formal logic or linguistic rigour to our everyday conversations we would paralyse the flow of meanings and anticipations that make sense of everyday interaction.

Everyday talk is inherently incomplete and it is our own practical reasoning that allows us to 'fill in' the truncated accounts that make up everyday talk. This practical reasoning is the shared understandings that participants bring to a communicative process (see Cicourel, 1971, pp.145-153). It is these crucial elements of common understanding that have to be borne in mind when analysing oral accounts in the office setting. It will be shown how they are embedded in wider interactive processes within the office world that have been the topic of discussion in previous chapters. The enquiry now turns to the rhetorical presentations of workers; that is, their oral accounts that display their competence and the circumstances of the case at hand. These simultaneous elements of talking about cases will be analytically separated in order to first draw out aspects of the 'good worker'. This will be followed by the way consumers are constructed in case talk. It will be shown that social work becomes visible in talk and that 'good' work can only be discerned by creating oral accounts based on the shared understandings that the competent member of the setting has acquired.

Telling the case: displays of the good worker

Oral displays are simultaneously an account about the consumers and the practitioners. While talk addresses private family lives it implicitly indicates practitioner skills and conformity to service ideals and assumptions. This process will now be separated to first deal with practitioner identities and relationships which inform the way talk is constructed and understood.

The following case concerns two teenage boys living at home but subject to a statutory supervision order in respect of minor thefts. In the supervisory process the worker sits and talks about her attention to the case. The family provides the unit of discussion and is unpacked through a description of family attitudes, relationships and behaviour. Within this journey through the 'family', the 'problem' is not specified as an item of clinical diagnosis. It is a hazy or non-defined property of the family that reveals itself in the conduct of one or more of the family members.

It will be seen that requests by the consumer for financial support are viewed by the worker as indicating a faulty perception of the service and an exploitative gambit; after all, clients are 'clients' because of insufficient moral, emotional and intellectual abilities. While this view prevails there is the dual identity of clients as unworthy but also redeemable; not yet in this higher state, but owning potential characteristics that may be improved by dint of the worker's persistence. The worker does not have to demonstrate her competence by linking her observations to some criteria of formal knowledge such as the skills and methods of practice. Similarly, she does not have to specify her efforts in relation to cures or outcomes. Instead there is a moral tale of family life detailing the client's departure from expectations held by the worker about appropriate domestic relationships. We join the following extract some half hour into the supervisory session:

team leader:	Right, lets move on to the next one (case).
child care worker:	Er, the Wells (groans from both participants). Dad's out soon, (from prison) that'll be a problem. David's on a job thing. (youth employment scheme). James is going to school. Mum's still unhappy, doesn't want me in. We had so much of a row the community copper came in to see me, 'everything OK Julie?' - 'yes thanks' I said (laughs).
team leader:	Is it just the supervision order that upsets them?
child care worker:	(pauses) *I've* (her emphasis) never *done anything* (ditto) for her, yes? When she wants bills paid *I've* (ditto) never helped. Other social workers have - you know that old one.
team leader:	Yes, it's a problem this one.
child care worker:	(nods) it's - 'they're my kids I don't want them supervised by anyone!' When you look at the file all the help has been material and that's not the way I work.
team leader:	Right, now the focus has changed - so has her attitude?
child care worker:	Well, she likes some workers and doesn't like me. The only way she likes a social worker is for money for bills.

team leader:	In a way it's healthy - she cares for the kids.
child care worker:	Yes, she's funny, she (softening her voice) she phoned up to say she was taking the kids on holiday and wanted to tell me where they were going and what they were taking, she certainly does her best for them....

So far, it is evident that both participants are familiar with the case. The worker proceeds quickly through the family members and situates the mother in a well known seam of clients who will invoke the memory of previous workers to influence the service orientation. In response the worker refers to the written record (the 'file'). The records are a flexible source of firm or defeasible information. In this context the record is cited as a reliable datum of past intervention, and the worker thereby substantiates her own claim to deliver a service of her own preference. Her firm insistence that material support will not be forthcoming leads to a 'row' with the client. This does not reflect negatively upon the worker but is understood on the basis that clients must receive the service defined by the practitioner.

The service does not have to be specified in relation to a set of activities or timetable of precise events. The common sense logic of the task informs everyone that work proceeds where and when it can and with those who are prepared to cooperate. Like her colleagues the worker prefers to avoid using sanctions to enforce her attentions on the clientele but seeks a pragmatic solution to resistant consumers.

team leader:	I'm really concerned about the kids here, they need help but it's mother's attitude, but there's no doubt she loves them.
child care worker:	Yes, she's got a lot of strengths and I want to work on those once I've got a better relationship with the kids. But I can't do much with her attitude at the moment, um, they're loyal to her, really we ought to be working with the whole family here. I don't want to go back to court with them, that won't do any good. The only way is to see the kids in the office.
team leader:	Right, let's see how it goes...

The case discussion is couched in the relaxed ordinary discourse of habitués and is rooted in the taken for granted assumptions that participants share. Their conversation maintains a subjective reality (Berger and Luckmann, 1967, p.172) by virtue of the routinised ways of understanding work which maps out past and future courses of action. For example, the social worker does not have to specify the 'problem' or the need to persist with a service or define the nature of that service. Like the health professionals observed by Strauss *et al.,* (1964, p.311) the participants are not required to make explicit reference to what they will actually do. Rather, there is an 'understanding' or a tacit acknowledgement that certain practices will continue, and that certain decisions or issues will be determined in due course. Thus the team leader completes the discussion with 'let's see how it goes', without clarifying 'it' or elaborating future arrangements and practices.

Good work is seen to have occurred when the worker shows she can dismantle the 'family' through descriptions of private lives and relationships. This act of telling the case cannot be treated simply as some verbalisation of past events such as the actual encounter with clients but is itself an entirely new act. Here the worker not only refers to the encounter but displays her own understanding and unique construction of events as she alone perceives them. The account is an occupational reality; a way of seeing families construed with regard to supervisory expectations and the worker's own interests. In this respect telling the case is work. It is an occupational practice that requires skill and experience and has to be properly conducted in order to accomplish an occupational identity. For an appropriate account indicates the practitioner to be the 'right sort of person' working in the 'right sort of way' and hence the worker may expect her definition of events to obtain.

The worker shows she is the 'right sort of person' through talk, that is, she displays her properly motivated conduct in routine oral accounts. The social worker does not establish the grounds for her activities by invoking some formal criteria or independent source of reference. Instead, she appeals to and manipulates the routine, shared assumptions within that particular setting. This is a feature of routine interaction in general (see Mills, 1940). We do not typically grasp the motivated conduct of those we routinely mix with by demanding 'reasons' or 'justifications' for their activities. Instead, we understand behaviour in respect of expected conduct in the ordinary verbalisations people provide about their everyday courses of action (see Ditton, 1977, p.148-9). In this sense, we understand peoples' motives in the context of their specific identities and accounts and through these we make sense of past and future behaviour.

Thus, the supervisor in the area office does not plumb the depths of the worker or her occupational skills in order to assess her motives. Instead, she and the worker rely on routine accounts about cases to establish that the worker is properly motivated. The social worker does not have to 'prove' she is dedicated, caring and competent, rather, it is assumed by the supervisor that only a worker motivated by these ideals can produce detailed accounts of clients' lives. It is within this everyday case-talk about families that practitioners indicate implicitly that their conduct is properly motivated.

To repeat, when the worker provides explicit descriptions of the domestic lives of the clientele, she implicitly indicates attention to service ideals. In this way discovering motives is to formulate the common-sense theory surrounding routine practice. Establishing motives is not a request for some official catechism but a request for a satisfactory answer to the routine query at hand (see Strauss, 1977, p.50-3). Thus the competent worker shows she is a 'good' worker by giving a 'good' account; that is, one versed in the common understandings of the setting. It follows that a demand for an account or an explanation of practice is a demand for the worker to exercise her common-sense theory of doing work.

It is through the experience of doing work that colleagues and clients become recognisable, specific and predictable relevances susceptible to routine management. For example, it is taken for granted that clients are 'clients' because they are inadequate parents and/or have disturbed or delinquent children. They receive a service in which the worker defines the relationship and locates the problem within their domestic network. In the extract below the worker employs this member-knowledge to make sense of an atypical consumer by standardising her behaviour in line with routine assumptions about the clientele. The worker appeals to the idea that problems lie 'beneath' the presenting phenomena of client lives, but like her colleagues she is reluctant to unearth the 'roots' of the unspecified 'problem' as this would demand more time and energy than she could spare. Consequently, the case is defined by the worker as presently stable but requiring further monitoring for the moment. It will be seen that the client wishes to terminate the relationship and the care order that concerns her child. The worker considers that this is not in the best interests of the mother and child but she does not make this apparent to the mother. Instead, she proposes a particular manoeuvre that will not disclose her opinions to the client and will ensure a continuing access to the family:

child care worker:	Yes, now this one (case) on Mrs. Barret. She's a difficult woman, resents social workers coming in.
team leader:	Yes she's lucky the child isn't acting out more.
child care worker:	She's a lovely little girl, tidy, pretty, plays quietly.
team leader:	We could revoke the care order but to do this she's got to open up a bit more, is that how you see it?
child care worker:	Yes, she's a very middle class lady (turns to me) we don't get many of those (laughs). Er, everything's underneath, lot of guilt underneath we should work with. But yes, in a sense I'd revoke tomorrow. She's much the same as all our mums I visit. They want to know why do we bring up the past. I said to Mrs. Barret that her daughter had been fostered for many years and is now back with her and these things can be a problem, er, getting adjusted. You see she wants her child to be perfect and that's not fair to the kid.
team leader:	OK what are you going to do on this one?
worker:	Well I don't want to expose this lady to her own inadequacies and undermine her confidence. Things aren't too bad but I want to be able to stay close and keep an eye on things. She's like other mums in that she wants an end to the care order. I'll show I'm moving towards it, say I'm writing a report but spin it out. But there doesn't seem to be much point in digging up old problems. Let sleeping dogs lie on this one. (team leader nods, asks for next case).

In this extract, as in all others, the worker does not specify overtly her conformity to service ideals, use of skills or the outcomes of her practices. Both participants 'fill in' these unstated properties. Both know that clients are to be skilfully managed in their own 'best interests' and that good work exists when workers are 'in there'; that is, gaining access to the domestic world of the client. The worker's ability to 'spin out' the report is a practical gambit legitimated by the assumption that clients are not equal partners in the service, and so the worker's diagnosis may be properly withheld. Such assumptions do not require elaboration in case talk. This is because both participants are able to draw on a shared common-sense theory about clients in order to complete the unstated meanings in accounts. Meanings are also retrieved by drawing on the background knowledge that both possess of the other. This knowledge has been gathered in the course of conversations, meetings, crises, and the daily minutiae of interaction whereby colleague identities are revealed and progressively established.

Within the supervisory encounter participants easily construct 'agreements' about the issue at hand. Indeed it would be surprising as Strauss (1977, p.49) observes, if members who share the same 'explanatory vocabulary' could not arrive at much the same conclusions. Accounts occur in what may be described as a context of consensus (see Scheff, 1967); that is, members are oriented to the moment through a perceptual system that is usually capable of working out an agreed formula between participants. The negotiable nature of clients' identities allows colleagues to resolve the uncertain conditions surrounding practice. Members can wring out a suitable account of work because clients may be grasped through flexible understandings. Likewise the preferred belief in practitioner competence entails minimal scrutiny and an assumption of the worker's ability to define the appropriate service. In this way, telling the case resolves delicate issues regarding the evasive nature of service outcome and matters of practitioner competence. Thus the failure of intervention does not signify some shortcoming in the worker's abilities; in fact crises, or unwelcome events in the family are rarely interpreted as failures of intervention. Instead, they are usually cited as evidence of existing or new pathology within the family or its immediate network.

Within case talk the emphasis is upon what 'everyone knows' about colleague relationships and client identities. Accounts are stylised to the extent that telling the case occurs through a shared frame of reference about these properties. In order to display these core cognitions it is not possible or necessary to excavate the inner processes of individual perception. Instead the observer, like the individual member, must learn the shared methods of sense-making for it is only by a competent acquisition of this common-sense theory of the setting that the member demonstrates she is the 'right sort of person' doing the 'right sort of work'.

So far I have attempted to demonstrate the long-term interactive properties beneath the construction of accounts together with the members' interpretative processes within the actual encounter. Accounts vary in length and content, for example, when worker and case are well known the oral display is likely to be condensed and heavily elliptical. Accounts concerning new cases, or indeed accounts by new workers, will require detailed elaboration until both become established in the imagination of participants. Nevertheless, an account is constructed through a weave of interests. The worker wishes to display selectively issues that suit her processing of the case whilst the team leader wishes to support and subtly assess progress and attention to service ideals. Within this complex event the 'family' is always to the fore of case talk; it becomes the template formed by the above processes and simultaneously a means of grasping the identities and issues involved in satisfactory practice.

The family is the conversational unit of analysis and becomes a framework within which work is accomplished as a witnessable and appropriate activity. The notion of framework as defined by Goffman (1974) refers to a universal feature of social organisation. Here Goffman refers to primary frameworks as a system of articulated rules but more typically a diffuse way of ordering perception that provides:

....only a lore of understanding, an approach or perspective.
Whatever the degree of organisation, however, each primary
framework allows its user to locate, perceive, identify, and label
a seemingly infinite number of concrete occurrences defined in
its terms. (Goffman, 1974, p.21).

The framework which bounds the realm of talk, is the 'family' and the domestic circumstances therein. Thus while workers recognise material, cultural and class characteristics of the people they visit, these may be commented upon on the way to the 'real' issues of family relationships. While the framework creates an orderly, shared perception, actual conversation works away at categorising those properties of family life that will situate their behaviour, attitudes and motives within a typical seam of activities that belong to these 'sort of people'. The 'family' is a means of collecting and classifying significant occupational information. In short, it is a form of search procedure. All organisations must engage in search procedures in order to match their technology to the appropriate objects, be they raw materials or people (Perrow, 1967). The search for typical problems and routine responses is a matter of occupational concern for all complex technologies. This can be seen in hospital clinics (Bloor, 1976, p.53-55) and in welfare organisations (Kemeny and Popplestone, 1970). Yet a casework technology concerned with the vagaries of domestic and intra-personal problems defies a clear programmatic response. Consequently as Perrow (1967, p.196) notes, the 'problem' is often grasped through guesswork, hunches and 'unanalysed experience or intuition'.

The following lengthy extract exemplifies the way that the 'family' provides a hazy form of search procedure for the worker. In telling the case, the worker searches through all manner of family detail and impression to substantiate her view of the 'problem' and the service she wishes to deliver. In this respect the details of family life are forever hostage to the selective views and understandings of the worker and her occupational requirements. Thus accounts are never about what 'actually' occurred between worker and client whatever that might be. Instead accounts are an occupational reality, they are an ex post facto construction assembled around negotiable understandings, identities and relationships within the work world.

The extract now commences with a reference to the uncertain nature of working with clients because of the unpredictability of domestic crises. The case concerns a young girl subject to a supervision order in relation to shoplifting offences. The family have been 'on the books' for years, and while they have 'problems' these resist explicit definition or solution. Yet work continues and is seen to be appropriate because of the flexible understandings that may be attached to clients and their lives:

child care worker:	You've heard the latest developments? Well one month to the day of the supervision order she (daughter) went to Southtown, shoplifting. Again! Got caught. Gave a false name - a friend of hers! (laughs) Well they found out. Anyway she'll have to go before the magistrates up there. I shall be recommending a fine and continuation of the supervision order. I had misgivings about the supervision but I haven't now. Jackie needs our help. But the trouble with the family is that you're lulled into a false sense of security, and then they blow.
team leader:	Yes this has been the pattern for years.

child care worker:	Yes, back when Glenda was working with them there'd be a crisis and then everything would be hunky dory.
team leader:	Um, but they didn't accept her.
child care worker::	No, they're not very accepting. When things go wrong they scream for help. They've got this massive guilt thing which I believe is some sort of incest, which is why they avoid social services as much as possible. The family, er, the reason for the order is that it's imperative that a social worker goes in and has some sort of relationship with the girl and builds up trust with the girl. Er, I see the only basis of working with the family is working with the girl, getting her to trust us.
team leader:	Right. It has to be on a regular basis not just responding to their crises and going out there.
child care worker:	Right, it has to be on a strict basis, er, statutory.

A career of see-sawing stability and crises is easily wrought from the case history and locates the clients in a typical seam of families dealt with by workers. The most recent 'eruption' of shoplifting is not related to a specific cause but so far is assumed to be connected with family relationships. Significantly, the term 'incest' has been introduced but hangs in the conversation without qualification or elaboration. It is not attached to any specific member or behaviour but remains a feature of the occupational assumption that problems are disguised. Consequently hints, clues and unverifiable guesses pepper this account and others. Thus workers do not have to specify their every phrase or comment. As a matter of routine conversation they move to and fro across the family history selecting what conveniently comes to mind, confident that the team leader is able to gather the meanings and inferences that colour daily talk. Thus the worker does not have to elaborate the way she will work with the family nor the measures she will take to build up 'trust' with the young girl. As the extract continues below, it can be seen that the worker is able to provide a detailed description of the teenager and relies on the fact that her diagnoses and opinions about clients are for an occupational audience only:

team leader:	OK. So what are you going to do for Jackie?
child care worker:	Er, preventing crisis and mediating with the family and hoping to get everyone to see how it is - er, you see you have a situation here where Jackie goes off to baby-sit for an older friend and stays with her boyfriend there. Parents can't control this. As soon as they try to stop her up she goes and disappears. But as I said yesterday perhaps it will phase out anyway - you know - if you make it a challenge it will go on. You see Jackie will only do what she's told not to do. If you tell her to do something she won't do it. But she's a reasonable girl who'll do a lot of things off her own bat. Like she'll do school work at home - but, if someone suggested that, she wouldn't do it! So it's trying to introduce a softly softly approach into the family, so that the family see things in some perspective and see the girl's pathology for what it is. She's got a lot of positives. She's a personable girl, pleasant, bright girl. One queer quality is an incredible neatness - her school work is absolutely immaculate. You can't tell the difference between one page and another. Every word the same!
team leader:	Sort of obsessional?
child care worker:	(pauses) em, very tidy. Very tidy people. I don't know what she's got. She's certainly got it up there the application of graphics - she's a bright girl. Although she's a problem in school behaviour-wise she's likely to blow up. If she doesn't blow she takes quite a lot in. She does reasonably well in examinations, she's got so many

	positives, she's not a negative girl altogether.
team leader:	The criminal bit doesn't fit in with this part of Jackie does it?
child care worker:	Well she's a well known shoplifter - to the extent that a note comes up the house saying 'Jackie can you pinch me a pair of trousers will pay £2 for them'. She's well known in her circle at school as the top shoplifter.
team leader:	She's not far from becoming a labelled criminal?
child care worker:	She, er, yes. But her criminality is in (pauses) er, strange really, it's almost a mania. It has a quality about it that is almost psychologically driven. I don't know if that's the proper use of the term 'psychology', but - you know - the drive is there, er because of an abnormal psychology, there's something there.
team leader:	Um, how long has she been doing it?
child care worker:	Got caught for doing this years ago.
team leader:	But not much recently?
child care worker:	She hasn't been *caught* (her emphasis) so much! (laughs).

So far the worker has stated her aims are 'mediating' with the family, preventing crises and hoping to get everyone to 'see how it is'. The worker does not specify what she means by this or how it will be achieved. Instead, she documents her intentions and abilities in the context of the drama and difficulties of family relations. The team leader recovers the full relevance of the worker's attention to service ideals because the account 'proves' the worker has established a relationship that reveals varied and intimate detail of client lives. As in all accounts, the family is the central topic. The worker unpacks aspects of the family that demonstrate the 'problem' although the precise aetiology remains uncertain. Witnessed or suspected faults, peccadilloes and clues are selected and emptied out as conversational jig-saw pieces to be mulled over. The girl has been known to shoplift, and as the extract indicates, the worker suspects this to be persisting. Accounts in this respect provide a means of 'status forcing' (Strauss, 1977, p.76). That is, behaviour is grasped on the basis of an identity that encompasses and confirms all manner of potentially uncertain activities. Thus, the girl is a client and it is safe to assume therefore that her conduct is continuing to be problematic. Similarly, while the girl is seen as academically able, her efforts in this direction are capable of reinterpretation and her handwriting provides yet another clue to an uncertain pathology. Yet like most accounts, the family and their membership are rarely cast as utterly unworthy. They have 'positive' qualities that intersperse the commentary and testify to their redeemable character.

The struggle between the antinomies of the client identity is forever present as case talk is essentially a moral journey through the family biography. However, it is the negative landmarks that are most prominent in the telling and logically so, given the members' common-sense view of clients' family lives as a realm of departure from normative expectations and responsibilities. The family is the proper focus of talk. Hence the girl's association with her peers and the impact of this upon her behaviour does not find a significant location in the search for meaning. The team leader reinforces the 'family' as follows:

team leader:	Yes, there's something *there* (her emphasis) in the family.
child care worker:	Um, very much, dad was an alcoholic ten years ago. Mother's a diabetic. You see the strange thing about it all is she (Jackie) has two other sisters. Mary is ESN, they've found a niche for her at (special school), settled in quite well. The youngest had a school report which I didn't see but mother told me, and mother doesn't usually lie - she hides the truth but she doesn't actually lie - has A's in everything so she must be quite bright and the other girl is quite bright. So you see there's lots of intelligence in the family which is quite a sort of solid, working class family. Mum's bright, it comes from her. Mum's background is better than what she's got, but the kids are immaculate, lovely kids really, (pauses) er, father, father's a weedy little creature, the original weed.
team leader:	Natural father?

child care worker:	Natural father, um. I know it's not relevant - he always wears black and white bri-nylon polo neck jumpers which is a strange thing for a man (pauses) and smart trousers, but he does nothing. He doesn't work - he's home to look after mum (wife) but he doesn't fiddle, like the bloke *could* (her emphasis) earn on the side but I'm sure the family are long term sup-ben (social security). Er, you support things, the three kids and wife, well over the years things erode away, you can't build things up when curtains get tatty, they don't get replaced, you need a new carpet you can't afford one, this sort of thing.
team leader:	Have you looked into the financial side?
child care worker:	No, I'll have to do that. I would say that if there's anything to be got they would get it. He looks after the wife and I think gets all that's going.

Telling the case involves this unfolding tale of family life. Accounts are in this sense a search procedure and the disparate elements of domestic relations tumble out in the telling. These details are implicitly structured by the 'family' as the source of 'problems' and 'pathologies'. Truncated and unexplicated descriptions are managed on the basis that 'everyone knows' that clients come from disorganised homes and their problems remain disguised and resistant. Indeed, the more recondite and mysterious the clues the more it 'proves' that the 'problem' is 'in there' somewhere. Thus in the above extract the father is identified as a potential source of the family's difficulties. This connection is not demonstrated other than by reference to the matter of his physical, sartorial and attitudinal departures from the worker's expectations. For example, the worker expects clients to 'fiddle' while receiving state benefits and the fact that the father does not supplement his income in this way is not deemed a laudable act but another example of his deficiencies. Thus, whatever a client may think of his or her own actions these are forever hostage to occupational understandings whereby all manner of conduct may be categorised as 'evidence' of the unspecified problems that colour family life. In this case, as in others, material difficulties are seen as exacerbating the domestic situation rather than a prime source of family problems. In the extract above the worker employs a sense of class structure but this does not interfere with the 'family' as the centre of her diagnostic concern. The infinite details of family life collect into a mixture of guesswork, hints and witnessed conduct that is interpretively malleable. The team leader once again interjects reaffirming the routine framework of analysis:

team leader:	Um, this is a pretty claustrophobic family - home all the time?
child care worker:	This is what I've said all the time, three girls, this little man, they're all in the back room. It's not a large house - he's not a constructive man - he doesn't use his time as far as I can tell to do anything - like for instance the curtains have been down from the front rail and that's been down for eight weeks, well he has the screws or nails you know. The house is not untidy, the curtains are washed and ready to be put up but it's just not done and whenever I go there he's just sat watching TV. Er, strange negative man, hardly any male lead to his daughters whatsoever - pathetic male figure and if there's any suspicion of incest it would only add to it. She's (mother) unfortunate looking, pleasant personality and smiling but she's a small dumpy woman can't afford to dress and they don't go out anywhere - but she's a fat happy body. She's not deceitful but covers up what suits her and she criticises us like hell - not to my face - and she'll say 'I've been trying to get hold of you for ages', the implication is you're never there when you're wanted.
team leader:	I suppose in that situation little things can blow up?
child care worker:	Oh right! You see, they see me as someone to be put up with, poking my nose in - that comment comes from

173

mother. But, I've had to get in there. Glenda (previous worker) didn't, no disrespect to Glenda, she's a very direct social worker, calls a spade a spade and will actually say to the family you're doing this wrong or this wrong. With all due respect I wish I could work like that but I can't, this is the feeling I get from clients - she was very direct. Now, she couldn't get anywhere with Jackie - that's not Glenda's fault, that's the way she works. But you see, school's the same they can't control her but then they can't control half the kids we deal with. What I'm doing is continually chipping away at the family, because the dynamics are not that bad - they're a criminal family, you know, in a criminal culture. They collude with Jackie's stealing but I wouldn't get my foot through the door if I accuse them of colluding with Jackie.

This cascade of domestic details indicates that the worker has made assiduous observations within the appropriate frame of 'family'. Her oral search through the family tacitly locates the daughter's conduct (shoplifting) as a problem to be grasped in the context of family roles and relationships. The extract reveals how workers perceive the clientele through a kaleidoscope of occupational and personal views of appropriate domestic arrangements. In this instance the 'father' has departed from the worker's notion of an assertive male figure providing a model of industrious, capable provider within and without the home. 'Mother' too fails to arrive at the worker's expectations about appearance and moral rectitude of a female parent. But then the parents are 'clients', these are taken-for-granted problem-people, potentially exploitative and dissembling. The mother, while not deemed 'deceitful' nevertheless attempts to 'cover up' and inhibit the worker's investigations. Indeed, mother's attempt to influence the service and criticise the worker is an instance of her inappropriate conduct and can be added to the pile of accumulating difficulties associated with the family.

It is important to re-emphasise that telling the case provides scant detail of 'how' the worker actually manages the encounter with clients.

Descriptions of family life, however phrased, rarely include the worker's own behaviour and demeanour when in the presence of consumers. This is assumed to be the sensitive presentation of a caring and capable professional. That this may not convince the consumer can be discerned in the above observation that a previous worker (Glenda) was unsuccessful in gaining access to the family. The present worker recognises that her predecessor employed a style of intervention that failed to gain entry to the family's private life. This is no occasion for criticism by the present worker who emphatically justifies her predecessor's preferred mode of practice. Thus the notion of collegial competence remains intact, and any 'failure' is cast within the family itself who will exclude a worker who confronts them openly with her opinions and requirements. As the worker states, she will be 'chipping away' slowly in order to maintain access and avoid hostility. This patient strategy is assumed by both participants to be beneficial and, as the following extract indicates, the time-table and content of future intervention requires no elaboration and is largely left to the worker to determine and define:

child care worker: You see there's the supervision order on Jackie, this gives me an 'in' with the other children. Mrs.(mother) I think is determined that the girls don't go the way of Jackie, she's given up with Jackie. Jackie will do what Jackie wants to do. I don't see the supervision as directive but supportive, Jackie can't be directed.

team leader: But you'll be seeing her on a regular basis?

child care worker: Monthly. Well I haven't worked this out yet. I must confess I haven't organised this yet but I feel it will need about monthly unless something happens, and working with her friend the babysitter as well, who's been involved with the shoplifting, and that's about it.

team leader: (turning to me) you can see the reasons for this supervision order, it's quite a task here mainly one of accepting social work.

175

child care worker:	Yes, you have to do this on the basis this is quite a delinquent family, we're not going to change that fact of their life style - it's cultural - I'm not going to change this you know - I don't intend to - the idea is to get Jackie through school into work and independent before there's a breakdown and she ends up in care, because no way is Jackie residential material. Care (residential) won't help Jackie one bit because home is so strong and the links are strong, basically because of mother's strength, but she's been close to care.
team leader:	Right then, you're on your way with this one, what's next....

The above extract concludes the case-talk surrounding Jackie and her family. The worker proceeds with other cases, other children and other parents. Child care social work is understood, assessed and 'seen' within accounts that are structured like the one above. The workers provide stories of family life made up of incidents, observations, clues and curiosities. Parents, siblings, friends, and relatives are decanted. The worker proceeds through family networks, relationships, biographies and behaviours. These are ransacked in order to find items that may have varying connection to 'problems' that are diffuse and largely undefined. Thus in the above case the 'shoplifting' is a symptom of family disorders. Suspicions, intuitions and all manner of domestic manifestations are raised and suspended. These are connected by unstated assumptions about clients and their problems. Thus 'incest' is raised but resides isolated in the account, it is implicitly 'in there' amongst the opaque relations of private family life. Incest is added to the collection of hunches and clues such as clothing, curtains, neatness, appearances, handwriting and psychological drives. All manner of selections are culled into a loosely connected backcloth which makes sense of the case and the worker's endeavours.

Workers do not articulate their exact practices, it is sufficient to say only that one will continue to 'work with' parents and children. Of importance to the supervisor is not the worker's preferred mode of working with clients, whatever that may be, but where she focuses her efforts and how she is motivated. The good worker applies herself to the family's private life. In doing so she must create a relationship that will extrude the details of domestic life. Such a relationship will only succeed in eliciting this information if it is 'caring', and the ability to persist in the exploration of problems despite resistance merely confirms the worker's caring dedication. Everyone knows that the job is replete with uncertainty. Problems resist identification, efforts fail, families move into crisis and there is never enough time to unearth the 'real' problems that lie beneath the crust of visible family life. Yet the worker, through soundings, brief forays and observed insights into family relations, can build a mosaic of suspicion that confirms the presence of 'problems' without specifying the precise cause or cure. This is sufficient to display appropriate practice. Fresh pieces are added to the family story as the case is discussed over time and as cases move in and out of stability. This after all is social work: the continuing patching up of family life, a worthwhile job carried out by dedicated workers for worthy people. Alternatively, it is a skilfully managed relationship with a difficult clientele, delivered by hard-pressed practitioners. Social work resides within and between these antinomies, forever indeterminate as situations change and members call forth the flexible and contrary meanings that resolve the uncertainties of the daily work.

Summary

Social work is an inherently uncertain enterprise. Lacking a sense of public esteem, facing unpredictable demands and without a clear and effective technology, the workers look inwards towards themselves. They socially organise their world through a common-sense theory that emerges from experience and maps out the identities and relationships of a complex work world. They make their work and themselves 'visible' through oral accounts structured by a complex weave of processes. The competent member routinely accomplishes work through an awareness of the background assumptions and interpretative procedures shared in the setting. For example, the worker learns the negotiable nature of formal rules and procedures, the implausible search for successful outcomes, the interpretively flexible motives and identities of the client, the moratorium on colleague criticism and finally the worker's own ability to apply a skilful discretion in the way she presents herself to both colleagues and consumers.

Accounts are constructed within this complex interplay of occupational assumptions. However the everyday nature of talk obviates any explicit reference to these assumptions that guide routine conduct. Accounts, albeit of varying length and descriptive detail, implicitly connect participants to the interests, motives and identities of both colleagues and consumers.

While these remain routinely unexplicated they are nevertheless completed by the competent theorist of the common-sense world. In this respect telling the case is itself a skilled practice accomplished by capable members; it is 'work' in a double sense. It is a complex construction in its own right; it also stands for all intents and purposes as 'work' in relation to unobserved encounters.

It could be argued that what actually happens between worker and client in the unobserved encounter is ultimately unknowable in the office setting, for the actual moment of client-worker interaction has no singular meaning - it is hostage to the varying understandings of the respective parties. Yet my concern here has been to show how this singular occupational reality, the encounter with clients, is constructed to make work a visible and orderly event. To this end, it has been shown that the unobserved encounter finds its meaning *in* the office setting, for it is here that work is 'witnessed' and assessed. In this sense, accounts *are* work, they are the routine means of 'seeing' the client and the worker. Good work can only be seen through a good account, one that maintains the framework of family and provides detailed pictures of domestic life. Satisfactory work requires an appropriate account, and a satisfactory account is itself an artful practice by a competent member. Work can only be substantiated and tested in the oral displays provided by workers. Thus whatever actually occurs 'out there' in moments of intervention has no direct bearing on the way work is symbolically constructed and thereby socially organised. Work is understood and seen in relation to processes outlined above and in previous chapters. These structure accounts and provide an occupational reality that is continually maintained in the conversational work of competent members. In this sense, social work is accomplished in the setting. That is, it is made visible, real, a predictable and proper activity within office. The logic and motives of the job exist here in the mundane work world and not simply in the formal theories of the profession, nor in the views of professional welfare theorists who eagerly pronounce on the impact and propriety of contemporary social work.

End note: looking to the future

child care worker: This chapter still feels familiar today. We still tell the case as you say, but not like they did, we're more into facts, where's the kid's needs, what are we doing about those needs? It's not as meandering, sort of open ended like in the chapter, it was like that before, now it's sharper. A lot of it (chapter) still stands up but a lot is history now. We're sort of tighter, more focused, more regulated. But I'm not sure if we or the families are much happier for it. It seemed a lot more relaxed and trusting then, but those days have gone. Also, the chapter has none of today's dilemmas. We are supposed to be more partner-like with users yet we do more control and intervention, we are supposed to empower but we do surveillance, we are supposed to keep the child with the family if we can but we don't have enough resources. There's a lot more contradictions in what we do that weren't there before and there's been change after change since your book....

Others in the office gave similar comments. The world had of course changed and such change no doubt had a unique history due to the particularities of this organisation and its personalities. Yet such changes have been visited on social work more widely, in this sense the office is something of a microcosm of the way child care has been transformed in recent years. Social work and its core project around families has become more closely defined and administered around child protection, at the same time the structure and culture of child care has increasingly come to be seen as producing a deep sense of insecurity and fear of blame, rather than any collateral rewards around self esteem and professional pride. Such a view, now commonplace in the occupational literature, is not the whole story. For example the staff described here were, despite their various tribulations, able to retain a degree of autonomy around work consistent with their judgement of what was safe to share or to retain cautiously under their control. They were self regulating over aspects such as anti-discriminatory practice. But more than anything else, they retained a formidable commitment and diligence towards the occupational task of child protection and to the much less well resourced field of family support. That the office did not wallow in some collective paralysis, acrimony, or other diversion in the face of an endless tide of referrals had much to do with the professionalism and quality of this much pressed colleague group.

The organisational and professional issues outlined in previous chapters will be familiar to a readership which has followed the lengthy debate around the shift in child care to a more interventionist stance. This debate needs no rehearsal here and rather than conclude with some nostalgic glance backwards in order to accuse the present, it might be more helpful to consider briefly the organisational and occupational future of workers such as these. In doing so, it will be suggested that in facing the challenges that lie ahead for social work we need far more research into the social organisation of practice which can make visible the ways in which providers and users of welfare establish their respective identities, needs, and solutions to private and public problems.

Looking forward

What we have seen over the last decade in human service professions is a shift towards more managed, efficiency driven, consumer led and effectiveness oriented service systems. This has been part of a slow but long running drift in public welfare culture and practice. In social work it has been accelerated and at times complicated by the upheavals brought by the Children Act 1989, the NHS and Community Care Act 1990 and local government reorganisation in Wales and England in the mid 1990s. Such far reaching changes are not over and at the time of writing there is much debate within a health and welfare policy elite over the possible disbanding of local authority social services departments and their dispersal in different task centred teams across, for example, health, education and the voluntary sector. There is, as the organisation gurus observe, only change ahead.

For social work the loss of a local authority organisational home may not be as critical as the loss of identity and a clear remit. In any event, the sweeping away of the sacred in professional practice is not a new experience for many in social work. More taxing will be the challenge of the fluid and unfixed in organisational life and its implications for some essential security over the function and purpose of social work.

We have seen from the workers' viewpoints above and in previous chapters that there has been a move in the last decade from a more diffuse ethic of care to a more careful watchfulness, from relationships as the means and ends of welfare to child safety as the abiding concern. Now, we have case management (intended or de facto) in child care that, in many areas, operates within smaller departments than before due to the recent reorganisation of local authority boundaries. But small is not beautiful when risks abound and where size counts decisively in delivering critical mass around resource flexibility and psychological well-being for staff. Yet a small, empowered, well motivated and flexible workforce that thrives on change has for some time been touted by organisation theorists as the successful work setting of the future. Social work has seen its fair share of change and has survived remarkably well, but operating effectively in small, resource constrained units in conditions of stress (that will always flow from protection work) will be a difficult trick to pull off. And change for what? What sort of child care social work?

If we were to be optimistic we could assume a service that is outcomes and effectiveness led in relation to policy goals likely to promote the best health and welfare for a democratic citizenry. If this were so, we could at least begin to itemise and aggregate some clear notion of the professional project. But that might be too naive or rationalist a response. For social work, as we have seen in these chapters, has to juggle all kinds of countervailing expectations - to make children safe yet strive to preserve the family, to empower yet intervene, to calculate risks and avoid mistakes yet operate in an inherently uncertain environment. And all in a time of limited resources and increasing bureaucratisation around case management. It would be unwise to believe that such contrary demands will somehow dissolve through any new administrative revolution in the organisation of statutory child care. Assume the irrational and expect the impossible. This may not be an implausible motif for contemporary child care social work in the UK. It has faced and continues to face in many directions. As a profession it remains anxious of the future and unsure of what aspects of identity and purpose may be solid and enduring.

It would not be difficult to enjoin with others in some dispiriting discourse on the end of welfare when what is urgently required of social work is determination and belief in itself. It is clear that child care has changed to a much more specialised and mechanised activity as intimated in the addenda to earlier chapters. But that does not adequately describe the people and events that constitute the occupational settings in which staff such as those described here practice. We need more analysis of the much neglected social world of welfare in order to understand how practice is constructed and how it can be changed. For, if social work has to reinvent itself to meet the world of constant change then it will be done in large measure through the capacities of staff such as those described here in collaboration with professional representatives, major employers and user groups who, together, must claim some distinctive territory around the future home and identity of social work. Thus if the occupational future of welfare professions in advanced economies is working in smaller organisations in self directed task centred teams that, ideally, have a range of skills and where staff are valued and regularly re-trained, then social workers such as those depicted here, would adapt well to such a setting. They already possess many of the key attributes around team working, self regulation and a capacity for change. What they, and many others lack, is a sense of being valued and empowered to tackle problems in more flexible and innovative ways that suit local circumstances.

How then can social work anticipate and demonstrate its preparedness for such a future, how can it reinvent itself in order to display with conviction that it is a confident and effective profession? Such questions already fuel a heated debate within the profession. The debate swings from pre-millennial gloom over the coming demise of all that was once cherished in social work, to a quiet (if implausible) optimism that somehow, all that the new political masters of welfare in the late 1990s will ask for, is some remedial tinkering in the way services are delivered in order to make social work ready for the next century. This of course does great injustice to the many thoughtful arguments that abound within an occupational literature that in recent years has turned more than ever before to questions of professional identity and organisational territory.

Yet within this debate, it has been hard to detect the collective voice of social workers themselves, a voice that might describe how they have handled change and achieved new aims set for their occupation. If the future of social work is to be negotiated with a policy and political elite not fully convinced of its merits, then it is even more important to get across to those who will listen, some account of the commitment ethics and energy of practitioners such as those we have discussed here. As a source of wisdom and guidance on the possible limits of professional ambition their views are invaluable. They are, after all, delivering on the present imperfect agenda of child care protection. They can deliver on this even better in a more balanced and reasonably equipped project of change vis a vis family support. Today's practitioners such as those described here, need to be made more visible by their occupational and professional representatives so that significant others can see that they deserve respect for tackling the problems of family life in an occupational environment of paradox, scarcity and blame. That they do this and generally do it well should be brought more insistently to a wider audience of key policy makers. Being more

182

informed of the motivation and determination of practitioners such as those mentioned here, they would surely be persuaded that social work does own a distinctive identity and purpose and that it should look with confidence to the future.

Methodological appendix

The original material presented in the first edition of this book in 1987 and again in this text stems from research conducted for my PhD. The study involved a period of twelve months observing child care workers in two fieldwork teams in a social services department area office. All members of the teams were interviewed individually on four occasions over the twelve months. Other key members of the setting were also interviewed such as the area office manager and deputy, the office receptionist and area office training officer. A total of seventy-six interviews were audio taped and transcribed. Information from various organisational documents and records were collected but these formed a minor part of the data.

Research methods

The purpose of the research project was explained to all the above participants and their agreement was secured before the programme got underway. My research role was primarily 'participant as observer' (Gold, 1970, p.376). That is, a role of a familiar but not equal participant in the setting. I wished to be seen by the members as an 'acceptable incompetent' (Lofland, 1971, p.100) that is, someone to whom they could explain their actions without feeling threats to their status as competent practitioners. I made it clear that I was not there to evaluate them or their work but to understand their job from their point of view. I strove to maintain a warm but distanced relationship so as not to influence the typical ways in which relationships and routines were managed. Thus while I was inevitably part of the content of interaction I was observing I did not wish to alter the usual *forms* of interaction between the office members. I was there to note the process of interaction, not to engage in its construction.

During the initial weeks I was seen as something of an 'outsider'. As time progressed I came to be seen more as a 'local'. I took messages, made beverages and generally tried to be of practical help if the occasion arose. This was a mild form of reciprocation for the data I was gathering and it assisted in shifting my identity towards being seen as a regular and sometimes useful visitor to the office. Over the many months of observation I sat at a spare desk near the two teams and frequently took part in the ad hoc talk and easy banter of office membership. However, I could always withdraw into reading documents and case histories and allow the other members to carry on with their activities free of any direct involvement by myself. While reading secondary sources I would make notes on the subject concerned, but it would frequently be the case that I would also make notes on events around me (this type of subterfuge has occurred in other research: see Ditton, 1977, p.10). During the course of the research I did not declare to members that their every comment or activity was a potential source of data. I believe then and now that continual declarations on my part that I would be noting their routine conduct would have had a distorting effect on their behaviour and on the research relationship. On the occasions when I employed the tape recorder such as during interviews, supervision sessions and team meetings this was always made evident to the participants and their permission was sought. Permission was given on the condition that confidentiality would be maintained. Hence, there has been no mention of the identity of the office or the department or the localities in which these are based and the names of workers and clients are of course fictitious.

Ethical aspects

It might be considered that the above research technique of making unobtrusive notes on the behaviour of office participants raises ethical issues. For example, is this not somehow a form of spying? My reply would be that I did inform all participants at the outset that I was a researcher and wanted to learn how they managed certain child care cases. I also explained my role to all concerned stating that I wanted to look, listen, observe and ask them to clarify aspects of their daily work. This they agreed to do. I did not let them know every time I was about to make a note about their behaviour or interaction in the office (for the reasons stated above). It might be noted here that in our everyday life we all, at times, prudently hide our observations and feelings in order to accomplish the task at hand. In this sense it can be argued that observational research is itself an exaggeration of ordinary practice (see Ditton, 1977, p.10). More important in my view is

185

the belief that the findings of observational research should be presented in a way that preserves the anonymity and integrity of the subjects and follows in the tradition of committed scholarship. Lastly, it should not be forgotten that the consequences of social work intervention can have profound effects on the lives of children and their families. An explanation of the social processes involved has merit if it reveals what lies behind the official gloss and legitimations that are produced by all occupations to justify their practices.

The interviews

Throughout the period, I gathered impressions and ideas about office life through the method of observation. I was also able to gain glimpses and insights that were not often repeated in the course of routine interaction (e.g., collegial criticism). What was needed however was a more systematic enquiry into some of these areas through the use of interviews. The first interviews were carried out after two months in the setting. Here, I gathered data on the biographical background of workers. I also introduced questions about the organisation and how the members perceived their relationships with higher management and other related occupations. This emphasis upon external aspects of the office setting contained topics which I thought might be less sensitive than questions about team and colleague relationships. This more delicate area was broached in interviews after some four and a half months in the setting. I thought it necessary to immerse myself in the office milieu before probing issues such as supervisory encounters, consultancy relationships and forms of social control in the two teams. The third and fourth set of interviews addressed the topic of the clientele. Observation had thrown up a variety of matters to be explored. For example, the flexible presentation of self during client encounters, client typifications, financial and material aspects of service delivery and so forth.

The interviews were not conducted from a formally designed questionnaire. Instead, I applied Lofland's (1971, p.75-92) device of a check list of questions and this guided a structured discussion with each member. The interview guide was tested on practitioners I knew outside the setting. This helped assess the plausibility and natural flow of questions and topics. I did not simply put some bald enquiry to the members but phrased questions so as to probe, play devil's advocate and offer interpretations to see if my gathering perceptions were accurate. Each member was guided through the same topic areas. These would also include quickly inserted questions that sought elaboration of more recent observations and hunches.

Where possible, these would be re-ordered into the interview sequence to run logically, collecting around a particular topic.

The interviews were conducted in light of the advice, skills and problems noted in research methods texts (Strauss *et al.*, 1969; Dean *et al.*, 1969b; Argyris, 1969; Becker and Geer, 1970; Spradley, 1980) and took note of linguistic and para-linguistic dynamics (Argyle, 1978; Phillips, 1973). Consequently, it must be emphasised that the interview situation is itself a social event that, to an extent, is independent of the intended purpose and content of questions and answers. Interviews are temporal acts existing in time and place and do not reveal invariant properties of a setting. Nor is there an invariant correlation between the asking of questions and the giving of information. Both the perceptions of interviewer and interviewee about the other will influence their reactions to the event. Inevitably, the researcher faces the same problem as any member of the setting. That is, shared information will crucially depend upon the ability to be accepted and trusted.

It has to be remembered that social workers are veterans of the interview. They routinely interview and observe during their countless interventions with clientele. It is quite possible for them to manage skilfully their contribution to the research interview. Hence, it was essential to review responses in the context of a gathering understanding of individual team members and my observations of them in the office. Thus it was the observation of daily routines and the interplay of interview data that became a template for comparison and analysis. The study of routine conduct with its tacit, habitual, difficult-to-recall quality, requires the use of both observational and interview research methods. These methods, and the data they produce, complemented each other in a spiralling relationship that helped correct and redirect the enquiry.

Analysis

During the research period it was necessary to constantly re-order data and redesign the analysis as initial clues, ideas and themes became redundant. This was because the research process of lengthy observation and sequential interviewing gave rise over time to a more logical and coherent grasp of the background assumptions that underwrite everyday work. In order to analyse this emergent flow of data and integrate what appeared to be a number of disparate themes, my approach was inspired to a large extent by the work of Glaser and Strauss (1967; 1970). Here, the researcher engaged in qualitative research seeks to generate grounded or substantive theory. That is, the construction of concepts and their integration into a set of hypotheses for a specific empirical area. For example, the familiar work of Glaser and Strauss (1965) on dying patients was a 'substantive' area to be theorised. Substantive theory remains faithful to the setting and provides an analysis of that unique phenomenon. Formal theories are attached to the analysis depending upon their capacity to support and extend the theory of the specific empirical situation. The objective is to generate properties and working hypotheses and wed these to an integrated theory of the observed setting.

The first stage in creating substantive theory is to construct categories of analysis and cast incidents and events within these categories. For example it was observed that social work consumers are described by practitioners through negative and positive occupational rhetoric. Thus a category might be 'client types' and within this the various properties of client behaviour, identity and circumstances, could be collected and compared. Data is constantly compared in this way and the aim is to summarise their similarities and differences under a more abstract and collective memorandum.

The next step would be to compare categories and their contents with other summarised properties; cross referencing their connections. The idea here is to reduce the number of categories and provide more uniform properties of the setting. A brief example will help elucidate this strategy. Consider the management of clients by social workers. An analysis of this could not be undertaken without including a range of categories based on collected data. Thus one might include categories such as 'client type', 'occupational danger', 'professional status', 'definition of the situation'. Hence an analysis might start with the following working hypothesis:

> Workers perceive clients (category: client types) as a potential source of problems and stress (category: occupational danger). Such problems threaten the self image of the practitioner which members construct through shared assumptions about collegial identity (category: professional status). With these assumptions the worker is able to impose her view (category: definition of the situation) of client circumstances and resolve the issue at hand.

This set of propositions would introduce the analysis which would then 'unpack' the hypothesis by specifying the connections between categories. At the same time there would be a search for instances that might qualify or negate the connections drawn. The objective is to demonstrate the underlying uniformity and connectedness between categories. In this way, data are reduced and generalisations created when large topic areas are condensed into increasingly integrated propositions, as in the above working hypothesis.

The outcome of this type of research is not the testing of one or two hypotheses as in experimental designs. Instead, it is the collection of many observations in propositional sets which are clearly and logically related to each other. Substantive theory attempts to provide explanations but this does not suggest that the theory is 'correct'. Instead, it is forever receptive to new empirical findings that will reshape, improve, or overturn the original formulation. Substantive theory does not attempt to secure universally applicable theories of causation, instead it is more concerned with plausibly generating working hypotheses and indicating the underlying uniformities that make social organisation possible. In my original research the analysis of the area office was introduced by a series of working hypotheses that set out the topic to be discussed in each chapter. Thus topics such as administrative routines, collegial relationships and supervisory encounters were each introduced by a set of propositions that were subsequently dismantled to show the reader the concepts and connections that justified the hypothesis. For a full description of the methods, relationships, ethics and analysis that guided this piece of research, see Pithouse (1984).

Bibliography

Abrams, P. (1980) Social change, social networks and neighbourhood care, *Social Work Service*, 22, 12-23.

Anderson, D. (1978) Social work reports and the grammar of organisational reaction, *Analytic Sociology* 1, D07.

Argyle, M. (1978) *The Psychology of Interpersonal Behaviour*. Third Edition, Harmondsworth: Penguin.

Argyris, C (1969) Diagnosing defences against the observer, in McCall, G. and Simmons, J. (eds) *Issues in Participant observation: A Text Reader*. London: Addison Wesley.

Arluke, A (1977) Social control rituals in medicine, in Dingwall, R., Heath, A., Reid, M. and Stacey, M. (eds) *Health Care and Health Knowledge*. London: Croom Helm.

Atkinson, P.A. (1996) *Sociological Readings and Re-Readings*. Aldershot: Avebury.

Baird, P. (1981a) Last word, *Social Work Today*. 12, 8.

Baird, P. (1981b) Last word, *Social Work Today*. 12, 28.

Barclay, P. (1982) *Social Workers Their Role and Tasks The Report of A Working Party set up in October 1980 at the request of The Secretary of State for Social Services, by the National Institute for Social Work under the Chairmanship of Mr. P.M. Barclay*. London: Bedford Square.

BASW (1977) The social work task, *British Association of Social Work*. Birmingham: BASW.

Becker, H. (1972) A school is a lousy place to learn anything in, in Geer, B. (ed.) *Learning to Work*. London: Sage.

Becker, H. (1976) The teacher in the authority system of the public school, in Hammersley, M. and Woods, P. (eds) *The Process of Schooling: A Sociological Reader*, for The Schooling and Society Course at The

Open University, RKP in Association with The Open University Press. London: The Open University Press.

Becker, H. and Geer, B. (1970) Participant observation and interviewing: A comparison, in Filstead, W.J. (ed.) *Qualitative Methodology: Firsthand Involvement with the Social World.* Chicago: Rand McNally.

Becker, H., Geer, B., Hughes, E. and Strauss, A. (1961) *Boys in White: Student Culture in a Medical School.* Chicago: University of Chicago Press.

Becker, H. and Strauss, S.L. (1968) Careers, personality and adult socialisation, in Glaser, B. (ed.) *Organisational Careers.* Chicago: Aldine

Bennis, W., Berkowitz, N., Affinito, M. and Malone, M. (1958) Reference groups and loyalties in the Out-Patient Department, *Administrative Science Quarterly*, 2, 481-500.

Berger, P. and Luckmann, T. (1967) *The Social Construction of Reality: A Treatise in The Sociology of Knowledge.* Harmondsworth: Penguin.

Bishop, J. (1977) Organisational influences on the work orientations of elementary teachers, *Sociology of Work and Occupations*, 4, 171-208.

Bittner, E. (1967) Police discretion in the apprehension of mentally ill persons, *Social Problems*, 14, 278-292.

Blau, P. (1960) Orientations towards clients in a public welfare agency, *Administrative Science Quarterly*, 5, 341-361.

Blau, P. (1964) The research process in the study of the dynamics of bureaucracy, in Hammond, P. (ed.) *Sociologists at Work.* New York: Basic Books.

Blau, P. and Scott, W. (1963) *Formal Organisation: A Comparative Approach.* London: RKP.

Blech, G. (1981) How to prevent 'burn out' of social workers, in Martel, S. (ed.) *Social Work Practice in Family Service Units: Supervision and Team Support.* London: Bedford Square.

Bloor, M. (1976) Professional autonomy and client exclusion: a study in ENT clinics, in Wadsworth, M. and Robinson, D. (eds) *Studies in Everyday Medical Life.* London: Martin Robertson.

Blum, A. and Rosenberg, L. (1968) Some problems involved in professionalising social interaction: the case of psychotherapeutic training, *Journal of Health and Social Behaviour*, 9, 72-86.

Brewer, C. and Lait, J. (1980) *Can Social Work Survive?* London: Temple Smith.

Bryson, L. (1952) Notes on a theory of advice, in Merton, R., Gray, A., Hockey, B. and Selvin, H. (eds) *Reader in Bureaucracy*. New York: Free Press.

Bucher, R. and Stelling, J. (1969) Characteristics of professional organisations, *Journal of Health and Social Behaviour*, 10, 3-15.

Bucher, R. and Stelling, J. (1977) Four characteristics of professional organisations, in Blankenship, R.L. (ed.) *Colleagues in Organisations: The Social Construction of Professional War*. New York: John Wiley & Son.

Bucher, R. and Strauss, A. (1961) Professions in process, *American Journal of Sociology*, 66, 325-334.

Burns, T. (1955) The reference of conduct in small groups: cliques and cabals in occupational milieu, *Human Relations*, 8, 467-486.

Burns, T. (1961) Micropolitics: mechanisms of institutional change, *Administrative Science Quarterly*, 6, 257-281.

Carlen, P. (1976) *Magistrates' Justice*. London: Martin Robertson.

CCETSW (1976) Values in social work: a discussion paper produced by the working party on the value bases of social work, *Central Council for Education and Training in Social Work*. London: CCETSW.

Cicourel, A. (1971) The acquisition of social structure: towards a developmental sociology of language and meaning, in Douglas, J. (ed.) *Understanding Everyday Life: Toward the Reconstruction of Sociological Knowledge*. London: RKP.

Coser, R.L. (1961) Insulation from observability and types of social conformity, *American Sociological Review*, 26, 28-39.

Coser, R.L. (1964) Alienation and the social structure: case analysis of a hospital, in Freidson, E. (ed.) *The Hospital in Modern Society*. New York: Free Press.

Crabtree, D. (1981) Joining the professionals, (Letters), *Social Work Today*, 12, 9.

Currie, R.(1982) Centre points, *Social Work Today*, 13, 16.

Daniels, A.K. (1975) Advisory and coercive functions in psychiatry, *Sociology of Work and Occupations*, 2, 55-78.

Davies, M. (1972) The objectives of the probation service, *British Journal of Social Work*, 2, 313-322.

Davies, M. (1981) *The Essential Social Worker: A Guide to Positive Practice*, with an Appendix on 'Law and the social worker' by Caroline Ball, Barrister-at-Law. London: H.E.B.

Davis, F. (1977) Uncertainty and medical prognosis: clinical and functional, in Freidson, E. and Lorber, J. (eds) *Medical Men and Their Work: A Sociological Reader*. Chicago: Aldine.

Dean, J., Eichorn, R.L. and Dean, L.R. (1969) Limitations and advantages of unstructured methods, in McCall, G. and Simmons, J. (eds) *Issues in Participant Observation: A Text Reader*. London: Addison Wesley.

DHSS: Social Work Service (1981) A study of the boarding out of children, *Department of Health and Social Security: Social Work Service*. London: DHSS.

Dingwall, R. (1974) *The Social Organisation of Health Visitor Training*, unpublished Ph.D. thesis, University of Aberdeen.

Dingwall, R. (1976) Accomplishing profession, *Sociological Review*, 24, 331-350.

Dingwall, R. (1977) 'Atrocity stories' and professional relationships, *Sociology of Work and Occupations*, 4, 371-396.

Dingwall, R. and Eeklaar, J. (1982) *Care Proceedings: A Practical Guide for Social Workers, Health Visitors and Others*. Oxford: Blackwell.

Ditton, J. (1977) *Part-Time Crime: An Ethnography of Fiddling and Pilferage*. London: Macmillan.

Dunham, J. (1980) The effects of communication difficulties on social workers, *Social Work Today*, 11, 10-11.

Emerson, J. (1969) Negotiating the serious impact of humour, *Sociometry*, 32, 169-181.

Emerson, R.(1969) *Judging Delinquents: Context and Process in the Juvenile Court*. Chicago: Aldine.

Emerson, R and Pollner, M. (1975) Dirty work designations: their features and consequences in a psychiatric setting, *Social Problems*, 23, 243-254.

Emerson, R and Pollner, M. (1978) Policies and practice of psychiatric case selection, *Sociology of Work and Occupations,* 5, 75-97.

Erikson, K.T. and Gilbertson, E. (1969) Case records in the mental hospital, in Wheeler, S.(ed.) *On Record: Files and Dossiers in American Life*. New York: Russel Sage.

Fabian, J. (1983) *Time and the other: How Anthropology Makes Its Object*. New York: Columbia University Press

Freidson, E. (1975) *Doctoring Together: A Study of Professional Social Control*. New York: Elsevier.

Freidson, E. (1977) Disability as social deviance, in Freidson, E. and Lorber, J. (eds) *Medical Men and Their Work: A Sociological Reader*. Chicago: Aldine.

Freidson, E. and Rhea, B. (1977) Processes of control in a company of equals, in Freidson, E. and Lorber, J. (eds) *Medical Men and Their Work: A Sociological Reader*. Chicago: Aldine.

Garfinkel, H. (1967) *Studies in Ethnomethodology*. New Jersey:

Prentice Hall.

Geismar, L. (1972) Thirteen evaluative studies, in Mullen, E. Dumpson, R and Associates, *Evaluation of Social Interaction*. London: Jossey Bass.

Giller, H. and Morris, A. (1978) Supervision orders: the routinisation of treatment, *The Howard Journal of Penology and Crime Prevention*, 17, 149-159.

Glaser, B and Strauss, A. (1965) *Awareness of Dying*. Chicago: Aldine.

Glaser, B. and Strauss, A. (1967) *The Discovery of Grounded Theory: Strategies for Qualitative Research*. New York: Aldine.

Glaser, B and Strauss, A. (1970) Discovery of substantive theory: a basic strategy underlying qualitative research, in Filstead, W.J. (ed.) *Qualitative Methodology: Firsthand Involvement With The Social World*. Chicago: Rand McNally.

Goffman, E. (1952) On cooling the mark out: some aspects of adaption to failure, *Psychiatry*, 15, 451-463.

Goffman, E. (1968) *Asylums: Essays on the Social Situation of Mental Patients and Other Inmates*. Harmondsworth: Pelican.

Goffman, E. (1971) *The Presentation of Self in Everyday Life*. Harmondsworth: Pelican.

Goffman, E. (1974) *Frame Analysis: An Essay on the Organisation of Experience*. Harmondsworth: Penguin.

Gold, R.L. (1952) Janitors versus tenants: a status income dilemma, *American Journal of Sociology*, 57, 486-493.

Gold, R.L. (1970) Roles in sociological field observation, in Denzin, N. *Sociological Methods: A Sourcebook*. London: Butterworth.

Goldberg, E.M. and Fruin, D. (1976) Towards accountability in social work: a case review system for social workers, *British Journal of Social Work*, 6, 3-22.

Goldner, F., Ritti, R. and Ference, T. (1977) The production of cynical knowledge in organisations, *American Sociological Review*, 42, 539-551

Goode, W. (1957) Community within a community: the professions, *American Sociological Review*, 22, 194-200.

Goss, M. (1961) Influence and authority among physicians in an out-patient clinic, *American Sociological Review*, 26, 39-55.

Gould, D. (1981) Minefields and measurements, *Social Work Today*, 13, 14-15.

Gouldner, A. (1957) Cosmopolitans and locals: towards an analysis of latent social roles II, *Administrative Science Quarterly*, 2, 444-480.

194

Hammersley, M (1976) The mobilisation of pupil attention, in Hammersley, M. and Woods, P. (eds) *The Process of Schooling: A Sociological Reader,* for the Schooling and Society Course at The Open University. London: RKP in Association with The Open University Press.

Hardy, J. (1970) The knowledge base of professionalism with particular reference to social work, *Social Work,* UK, 27, 16-21.

Heraud, B. (1971) British social work: a profession in process, *Social Casework,* 52, 347-355.

Heraud, B. (1981) *Training for Uncertainty: A Sociological Approach to Social Work Education.* London: RKP.

Herstein, N. (1969) The latent dimension of social work research, *Social Casework,* 50, 269-275.

Holdaway, S. (1977) Changes in urban policing, *British Journal of Sociology,* 28, 119-137.

Hughes, D. (1977) Everyday and medical knowledge in categorising patients, in Dingwall, R., Heath, C., Reid, M. and Stacey, M. (eds) *Health Care and Health Knowledge.* London: Croom Helm.

Hughes, D. (1980) The ambulance journey as an information generating process, *Sociology of Health and Illness,* 2, 115-132.

Hughes, E. (1928) Personality types and the division of labour, *American Journal of Sociology,* 33, 754-768.

Hughes, E. (1951) Work and self, in Rohrer, J.H. and Sherif, M. (eds) *Social Psychology at the Crossroads.* New York: Harper.

Hughes, E. (1958) *Men and Their Work.* New York: Free Press.

Hughes, E. (1968) Career and office, in Glaser, B, (ed.) *Organisational Careers,* Chicago: Aldine.

Irvine, E. (1969) Education for social work: science or humanity? *Social Work,* UK, 26, 3-6.

Johnson, P.(1980) Judge in murder case gives warning to social workers, *The Guardian,* 22.1.80, 5, London and Manchester: Guardian Newspaper.

Kemeny, P. and Popplestone, G. (1970) Client discriminations in social welfare organisations, *Social Work,* UK, 27, 7-16.

Klapp, O.E. (1954) Heroes, villains and fools as agents of social control, *American Sociological Review,* 19, 56-62.

Lait, J. (1980) Social work knowledge: a case of inflation, in Anderson, D. (ed.) *The Ignorance of Social Intervention.* London: Croom Helm.

Lofland, J. (1971) *Analysing Social Settings: A Guide to Qualitative Observation and Analysis,* Belmont, California: Wadsworth.

Lorber, J. and Satow, R. (1977) Creating a company of unequals: sources of occupational stratification in a ghetto community mental health centre, *Sociology of Work and Occupations*, 4, 281-302.

Macdonald, M. (1966) Reunion at vocational high: an analysis of girls at vocational high: an experiment in social work intervention, *Social Services Review*, 40, 175-189.

Manning, P. (1971) Talking and becoming: a view of organisational socialisation, in Douglas, J. (ed.) *Understanding Everyday Life: Towards the Reconstruction of Sociological Knowledge*. London: RKP.

Manning, P. (1977) Rules, colleagues and situationally justified actions, in Blankenship, R.L. (ed.) *Colleagues in Organisations: The Social Construction of Professional Work*. New York: John Wiley & Son.

Manning, P. (1979a) The social control of police work, in Holdaway, S. (ed.) *The British Police*. London: Edward Arnold.

Manning, P. (1979b) *Police Work: The Social Organisation of Police Work*. Massachusetts: MIT.

Mattinson, J. and Sinclair, I. (in collaboration with Cousell, P. and Morley, R.) (1980) *Mate and Stalemate: Working with Marital Problems in a Social Service Department*. Oxford: Blackwell.

Matza, D. (1976) Signification, in Hammersley, M. and Woods, P. (eds) *The Process of Schooling: A Sociological Reader*, for the Schooling and Society course at the Open University. London: RKP in Association with the Open University Press.

Matza, D. and Sykes, G. (1957) Techniques of neutralisation: a theory of delinquency, *American Sociological Review*, 22, 664-670.

Merton, R. (1957) *Social Theory and Social Structure*. (Revised Edition). New York: Free Press.

Merton, R. (1968) *Social Theory and Social Structure*. (Enlarged Edition). New York: Free Press.

Meyer, C.H. (1973) Practice models: the new ideology, *Smith College Studies in Social Work*, 43, 85-98.

Meyer, J. and Rosenblatt, A (1975) Encounters with danger: social workers in the ghetto, *Sociology of Work and Occupations*, 2, 227-245.

Mills, C.W. (1940) Situation action and vocabularies of motive, *American Sociological Review*, 5, 904-913.

Moore, W. and Tumin, M. (1949) Some social functions of ignorance, *American Sociological Review*, 14, 787-795.

Mukerji, C. (1976) Having the authority to know: decision making on student film crews, *Sociology of Work and Occupations*, 3, 63-87.

Nurse, J. (1973) Client, caseworker and absent third person, *British Journal of Social Work*, 3, 210-227.

Olsen, R. (1980) Tables are turned on social work critics, *Social Work Today*, 12, 3.

Parsloe, P. (1981) *Social Services Area Teams*. London: Allen and Unwin.

Pearson, G. (1978) Social work and law and order, *Social Work Today*, 9, 19-24.

Pearson, G (1983) The Barclay Report and community social work: Samuel Smiles revisited? *Critical Social Policy*, 2, 78-86.

Perrow, C. (1967) A framework for the comparative analysis of organisations, *American Sociological Review*, 32, 194-208.

Phillimore, P. (1981) *Families Speaking: A Study of Fifty One Families' Views of Social Work*. London: Family Service Unit.

Phillips, D. (1973) *Abandoning Method: Sociological Studies in Methodology*. London: Jossey Bass.

Pinker, R. (1971) *Social Theory and Social Policy*. London: HEB.

Pinker, R. (1982a) Social work is casework, in Philpot, T. (ed.) *A New Direction for Social Work: The Barclay Report and Its Implications*. Surrey: Community Care/IPC Press.

Pinker, R. (1982b) An alternative view: a note by Professor R.A. Pinker, Appendix B in Barclay, P. *Social Workers Their Role and Tasks: The Report of a Working Party set up in October 1980, at the Request of the Secretary of State for Social Services by the National Institute for Social Work under the Chairmanship of Mr Peter M. Barclay*. London: Bedford Square.

Pithouse, A. (1984) *Social Work: The Social Organisation of an Invisible Trade*, unpublished Ph.D. thesis, University College Cardiff.

Plowman, D. (1969) What are the outcomes of casework? *Social Work*, UK, 26, 10-19.

Punch, M. (1979) The secret social service, in Holdaway, S. (ed.) *The British Police*. London: Edward Arnold.

Raffel, S. (1979) *Matters of Fact: A Sociological Enquiry*. London: RKP.

Raynor, P. (1978) Compulsory persuasion: a problem of correctional social work, *British Journal of Social Work*, 8, 411-424.

Rees, S. (1978) *Social Work Face to Face: Clients' and Social Workers' Perceptions of the Content and Outcome of Their Meetings*. London: Edward Arnold.

Robinson, J. (1971) Experiment and research in social casework, *British Journal of Social Work*, 1, 463-480.

Rose, G. (1957) Assessing the results of social work, *Sociological Review*, 5, 225-237.

Rosenblatt, A. and Meyer. J.E. (1975) Objectionable supervisory styles: students' views, *Social Work*, (US), 20, 184-189.

Roth, J (1964) Information and the control of treatment in a tuberculosis hospital, in Freidson, E. (ed.) *The Hospital in Modern Society*. New York: Free Press.

Roth, J (1968) The study of the career timetables, in Glaser, B. (ed.), *Organisational Careers*, Chicago: Aldine.

Roth, J. (1972) Some contingencies of the moral evaluation and control of clientele: the case of the hospital emergency service, *American Journal of Sociology*, 77, 839-856.

Roy, D (1952) Quota restriction and goldbricking in a machine shop, *American Journal of Sociology*, 57, 427-442.

Roy, D. (1953) Work satisfaction and social reward in quota achievement: an analysis of piecework incentive, *American Sociological Review*, 18, 507-514.

Roy, D. (1960) Banana time: job satisfaction and informal interaction, *Human Organisation*, 18, 156-168.

Ruzek, S. (1973) Making social work accountable, in Freidson, E. (ed.) *The Professions and Their Prospects*. London: Sage.

Sackville, A., Douglas, B. and Williams, T. (1978) Workload management, discussion paper, *British Association of Social Work*. Birmingham: BASW.

Sainsbury, E. (1975) *Social Work with Families: Perceptions of Social Casework Among Clients of a Family Service Unit*. London: RKP.

Sainsbury, E. (1980) Client need, social work method and agency function: a research perspective, *Social Work Service*, June, 9-15.

Satyamurti, C. (1981) *Occupational Survival: The Case of The Local Authority Social Worker*. Oxford: Blackwell.

Scheff, T. (1967) Towards a sociological model of consensus, *American Sociological Review*, 32, 32-40.

Scheff, T. (1968) Negotiating reality: notes on power in the assessment of responsibility, *Social Problems*, 16, 3-17.

Schutz, A, (1964) *Collected Papers II: Studies in Social Theory*, Brodersen, A. (ed.) The Hague: Martinus Nijhoff.

Scott, W.R. (1969) Professional employees in bureaucratic structure: social work, in Etzioni, A. (ed.) *The Semi-Professions and Their Organisation: Teachers, Nurses, Social Workers*. New York: Free Press.

Shearer, A. (1980) Is your social worker really necessary? *The Guardian*, 28.8.80, 16, London and Manchester: Guardian Newspapers.

Shibutani, T. (1955) Reference groups as perspectives, *American Journal of Sociology*, 60, 562-569.

Sinfield, A. (1974) Poverty and the social services department, in Brown, M.J. (ed.) *Social Issues and the Social Services*. London: Charles Knight.

Smith, G. (1980) *Social Need: Policy, Practice and Research*. London: RKP.

Smith, P.(1979) Social workers and the judges rules, *Journal of Social Welfare Law*, (March), 155-161.

Spradley, J. (1980) *Participant Observation*. London: Holt Rinehart and Winston.

Stevenson, O. (1981) *Specialisation in Social Service Teams*. London: Allen and Unwin.

Stevenson, O. and Parsloe, P. (1978) *Social Service Teams: The Practitioner's View*. London: (DHSS), HMSO.

Strauss, A. (1977) *Mirrors and Masks: The Search for Identity*. London: Martin Robertson.

Strauss, A.(1978) A social world perspective, in Denzin, N.K. (ed.) *Studies in Symbolic Interaction: An Annual Compilation of Research.* Volume I. Connecticut: JAI Press Inc.

Strauss, A., Schatzman, L., Bucher, R., Erhlich, D. and Sabshin, M. (1963) The hospital and its negotiated order, in Freidson, E. (ed.) *The Hospital in Modern Society*. New York: Free Press.

Strauss, A., Schatzman, L., Bucher, R., Erhlich, D. and Sabshin, M. (1964) *Psychiatric Ideologies and Institutions*. New York: Free Press.

Strauss, A ., Schatzman, L., Bucher, R., Erhlich, D. and Sabshin, M. (1969) Field tactics, in McCall, G. and Simmons, L. (eds) *Issues in Participant Observation: A Text Reader*. London: Addison Wesley.

Strong, P. (1980) Doctors and dirty work: the case of alcoholism, *Sociology of Health and Illness*, 2, 24-27.

Sudnow, D. (1968) Dead on arrival, *New Society* (February 8) 11, 187-189.

Syson, L with Baginsky, M. (1981) *Learning to Practice: A Study of Placements in Courses Leading to The Certificate of Qualification in Social Work*. CCETSW Study No. 3. London: Central Council for Education and Training in Social Work.

Tillich, P. (1969) The philosophy of social work, *Social Service Review*, 36, 13-16.

Titmuss, R. (1973) *The Gift Relationship: From Human Blood to Social Policy*. Harmondsworth: Pelican.

Van Maanen, J. and Katz, R. (1979) Police perceptions of their work environment, *Sociology of Work and Occupations*, 6, 31-59.

Walsh, J.L. (1977) Career styles and police behaviour, in Bailey, D.H. (ed.) *Police and Society*. London: Sage.

Walsh, J.L. and Elling, R. (1977) Professionalism and the poor: structural effects and professional behaviour, in Freidson, E. and Lorber, J. (eds) *Medical Men and Their Work: A Sociological Reader*. Chicago: Aldine.

Wasserman, H. (1975) Social work treatment: an essay review, *Smith College Studies in Social Work*, 45, 183-195.

Weber, M. (1948) *From Max Weber: Essays in Sociology*, in Gerth, H. and Mills, C.W. (eds) London: RKP.

Westley, W.A. (1970) *Violence and the Police: A Sociological Study of Law, Custom and Morality*. Massachusetts: MIT Press.

Whittington, C. (1983) Social work in the welfare network, *British Journal of Social Work*, 13, 265-286.

Wieder, D.L. (1974) *Language and Social Reality: The Case of Telling the Convict Code*. The Hague: Mouton and Co.

Wilkins, L. (1965) New thinking in criminal statistics, *The Journal of Criminal Law, Criminology and Police Science*, 56, 277-284.

Wilson, J.Q. (1978) *Varieties of Police Behaviour: The Management of Law and Order in Eight Communities*. Cambridge, Massachusetts: Harvard University Press.

Zimmerman, D. (1969) Record keeping and the intake process in a public welfare agency, in Wheeler, S. (ed.) *On Record: Files and Dossiers in American Life*. New York: Russell Sage.